FISHI WASATCH

Anthony Nelson

with

Contributions by Lewis Garrett

"Utah's Outdoor Guys"

ISBN: 1495393925
ISBN-13: 9781495393921

DEDICATION

This book is dedicated to all of the people who have dedicated their efforts, talents and treasury to protect the Wasatch Mountains from over development and to protect its unique wilderness characteristics.

The book is also dedicated to the men and women of the Utah Department of Wildlife Resources whose vision, hard work and stewardship of Utah's wildlife resources has provided all of the citizens of Utah and our country the opportunity to enjoy Utah's wildlife heritage.

SPECIAL THANKS

I would like to give thanks to Eric Bean and Wasatchhiker.com for all of their assistance with providing professional photos of many lakes covered in this book.

WasatchHiker.com is a hiking resource for people of all skill levels. It provides information on how to get started and where to go for some great experiences. The website contains a database of destinations, trails and trailheads, along with descriptions, photos, videos and statistics. A Facebook group page under the same name provides current conditions, hiking related news and trail reports.

CONTENTS

ABOUT THE AUTHOR

Anthony Nelson is an entrepreneur, author, business owner and avid outdoorsmen. He has helped many people realize their dream of business ownership. Together with his wife Jennifer, they founded and are owners of SHS Franchising. SHS Franchising is the parent company of Spectrum Home Services. Spectrum Home Services is a very successful home services business that was started in 2000 by both Anthony and Jenny. It was so successful that they chose to begin franchising the concept in 2004.

Anthony Nelson has written several articles for fish and game magazines and has written several books relating to both business and the outdoors. He also is the author of the Wild Forage blog found at Wildforage.wordpress.com

Anthony Nelson is a graduate of California State University Long Beach where he earned his degree in Political Science. He Lives in Draper Utah with his wife Jennifer and his two children, Jacob and AnnMarie.

BOOK GUIDES

As you read this book, you will notice pictures that are used as guides to indicate specific information about each of the lakes. The following is the list of picture guides and what they represent.

Drainage Map

Fish stocked by airplane

Fish stocked by truck

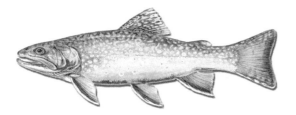

Fish species in the lake

Topographic map of area surrounding lake

1

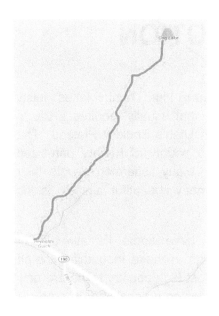

Trail Map image, trails marked by red line.

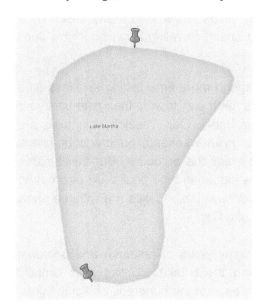

Productive fishing locations marked by red pushpins.

11

INTRODUCTION

To most fishermen, alpine fishing means high country lakes, feisty trout and incredible scenery. In Utah, that usually requires a trip to the Uinta Mountain range or southern Utah's Boulder Plateau. The mountain lakes found there provide a bounty of hungry pan-sized trout along with breathtaking scenery. Many fishermen devote their entire summer to exploring the many beautiful alpine fishing opportunities these areas have to offer.

These well-known fishing spots do have some limitations. For example, weather and snow pack. High in these mountains, ice-off comes late and winter comes early. Most high country lakes are only fishable from July to late September making it necessary to cram as much fishing as possible into this short period of time. Travel time is another critical factor. The prime alpine lakes of the Uinta and Boulder mountains involve long drives followed in many cases by a significant hike. Each hour you spend traveling is an hour you don't spend fishing.

How can a Utah alpine junkie spend more time fishing and less time traveling? Wasatch front anglers need only look to their own backyard for quality alpine fishing close to home. Our Wasatch Mountains are far from undiscovered, on any given weekend; hundreds of hikers and bikers take to the trails to enjoy the outdoors. But these same mountains and the pristine lakes hidden in their peaks are overlooked by most fishermen. Several productive alpine lakes are within a short drive and a day-hike from Salt Lake City.

This book is a culmination of many years of research and personal experience hiking to and fishing these lakes. Unlike the Uinta's, where it would take years to fish each of the hundreds of alpine lakes, the Wasatch alpine lakes are fairly close together and it is possible for avid fishermen (with a lot of time on their hands) to fish most of these lakes in a single summer season. If you are lucky enough to devote a summer to fishing these mountain lakes, you will have the honor of knowing that you completed the Wasatch Alpine Fishing Slam!

The purpose of this book is to give you the knowledge you will need to fish these lakes successfully. The maps, trail guides and topography maps are included for your information. However, these maps are not to scale and it is very important that you do not rely solely on these sample maps as a guide. There are books and guides that have been written for the sole purpose of detailing the hiking trails in the Wasatch Mountains. These books and guides can be found on the internet and in book stores. I would recommend that you purchase one of these Wasatch Mountain hiking guides as a complement to this book.

I would like to thank the Utah Division of Wildlife Resources (DWR) for all of the help and information they provided for this book. The Division of Wildlife Resources has a wealth of information for fishermen and I would recommend that all fishermen utilize their expertise. Often a phone call to the Division will result in first hand information about current conditions that will help make your trip a success. The dedicated men and women of the Division are there to help you.

In this book I will cover the different fish species that inhabit not only the alpine lakes but all of the sport fishing species found in Utah's many varied aquatic habitats. The book will also cover the animals that you may encounter when fishing the Wasatch. The Wasatch may be in close proximity to 2 million people but it is an island of very wild country with abundant wildlife diversity. There are many types of large and small mammals, reptiles, birds and other creatures that make the Wasatch their home and we need to realize that we are just guests. Respect these animals and give them the space they need.

I will also share my experience regarding the best types of equipment, lures, flies, bait and fishing techniques to help insure a successful fishing trip. These recommendations are based on my own research and knowledge of each lake. Please remember though that these lakes are always changing and are subject to drought, heavy winter kill, high water conditions, over population and a myriad of other issues that can affect your fishing and the effectiveness of my recommendations. Each lake will have a map highlighting where I have had the most success catching fish from that lake. Once again, this can change from year to year and even from day to day so be be willing to try other areas of the lake if the areas outlined in the book are not producing for you.

I have also included basic information about the lakes that don't contain any sport fish. They are included so you did not waste your time hiking to these lakes if fishing is your main purpose. I have already made those mistakes for you. However, if you would like to just hike to these lakes, the information on each of the lakes is here for your review.

Finally, the book provides information on Forest Service campgrounds. One of the nice things about the Wasatch lakes is that they are close to both the Salt Lake Valley and Utah Valley. For those so inclined, it is possible to stay in a campground and commute to work and then return in the afternoon and fish the lakes or streams near the campground. This is a great mini-vacation that is affordable and close. It is also a great opportunity to escape the summer heat in the valleys.

It is my hope that this book will open your eyes to the excellent alpine fishing opportunities so close to home. We are lucky to have such quality fishing and wilderness experiences in our back yard. It is up to us to make sure that these experiences are also passed on to future generations. When you fish these lakes please make sure that you leave no trace behind. No one likes to hike for several hours to

1

finally make it to their destination and see trash. If you do see trash, pick it up and carry it out. Everyone will thank you.

Make sure to get out this alpine fishing season and explore these wonderfully Wasatch Mountain Lakes and the great fishing. I hope to see you on a trail!

CHAPTER 1
Fish Species of Utah

WHAT LURKS BENEATH ALL OF THAT WATER ANYWAY?

There is nothing like catching a jumping brown in a beautiful little creek, a brilliantly colored Rainbow in a cool deep reservoir, a feisty cutthroat in a forgotten stream, a hungry Brook trout in a high mountain lake or a giant Tiger Muskie from the depths of Pineview Reservoir. In Utah, we are blessed with the opportunities to fish for these and other magnificent creatures year-round in the many different lakes and streams throughout the state.

TROUT SPECIES

In the past, when the word trout was mentioned in Utah it was usually preceded by the word Rainbow. The reason for this was simple, since the 1960's the official state fish was the **Rainbow Trout**, a non native species which made its way to Utah from its home waters on the West Coast. Rainbow trout are preferred by wildlife agencies for put-and-take fisheries because of the relative ease of raising thousands of these fish and their popularity amongst anglers. Utah anglers spend thousands of hours each year fishing the waters of this state in search of their limit of stocked Rainbows.

Rainbows are stocked in most Utah waters. The longer they have been in a stream or lake, the more acrobatic, defiant and beautiful they become. Colors vary greatly depending on habitat, size and maturity. Stream rainbows and spawning fish have more intense colors than Lake Rainbows. Rainbows found in lakes tend to be more silvery. A mature rainbow is dark green too bluish on the back with silvery sides. The reddish horizontal band gives the fish its name. The belly is usually white and black spots are present on the

1

head, back and sides. These fish are not sterile and can reproduce naturally. In many lakes that contain Rainbow and Cutthroat trout, the fish have interbred, producing a hybrid called the Cutbow.

*Fish illustration courtesy of the Utah Department of Wildlife Resources

With the increasing popularity of catch and release fishing and the escalating cost of hatcheries, there has been a shift in attitude by many anglers and wildlife officials. More attention is now directed to wild fish stocks and native fish species. In Utah, the only native trout species is the Cutthroat. The **Bonneville Cutthroat** is native to the streams and lakes in and around the Wasatch Mountains. Bonneville Cutthroat have sparsely scattered, very distinctly round spots over the upper body. They have subdued colors of silver-gray to charcoal on their upper body with subtle hues of pink on their flanks during the spawning season.

Bonneville Cutthroats are what the early Mormon Pioneers survived on during their first winter in the Salt Lake Valley. Some of the diaries of these early pioneers recorded incredible populations of these trout in Utah Lake and the streams of the Wasatch. Bonneville cutthroats in Utah Lake once weighed as much as 15 pounds and were so numerous that a commercial fishery was undertaken to provide fish to the early pioneers. But over-fishing, destruction of spawning streams, pollution and the introduction of nonnative species has reduced the population of these fish throughout the state. Sadly, the

Bonneville Cutthroats, once so numerous in Utah Lake, no longer ply its murky waters.

In recent years, pockets of pure Bonneville Cutthroats have been found throughout Utah. These waters are either closed to fishing or open to catch-and-release fishing with artificial flies and lures to help protect these populations.

The importance of Bonneville Cutthroat to Utah's heritage was underscored in 1997 when the state changed the official fish from the Rainbow to the Bonneville Cutthroat. The DWR has programs underway to reintroduce this native fish to many of the streams they once inhabited.

*Fish illustration courtesy of the Utah Department of Wildlife Resources

The Bear Lake Cutthroat is a strain of the Bonneville Cutthroat and it is sometimes hard to tell each of them apart. The Bear Lake strain often lacks the bright crimson jaw slash.

The Yellowstone Cutthroat was introduced into Utah early in the 1900's and has been the predominant subspecies used in management programs throughout the state. It is lightly spotted with distinctly round spots concentrated around the tail area.

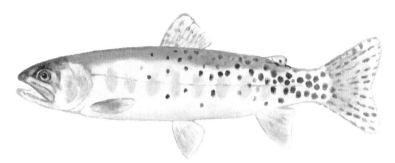

*Fish illustration courtesy of the Utah Department of Wildlife Resources

The Colorado River Cutthroat evolved in the Colorado/Green River drainage's and is noted for its brilliant coloration. The males, in spawning condition, have bright crimson stripes along their sides and their stomach is often crimson. The spots on this fish are concentrated around the tail section.

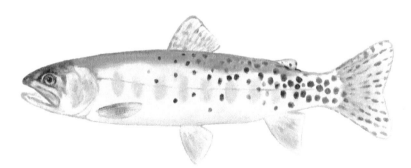

*Fish illustration courtesy of the Utah Department of Wildlife Resources

The Brown trout is a hardy fish, which can coexist and complete well with other species and they can also endure marginal water conditions better than most trout. Brown trout are not native to Utah and were introduced to the Americas from Europe. It generally has golden brown hues with a yellow underbelly and crimson spots circled with blue halos. The upper body of this trout is usually dappled with large dark spots. Large males during spawning will sometimes develop a hooked jaw. Brown trout can grow to sizes in excess of 10 pounds.

*Fish illustration courtesy of the Utah Department of Wildlife Resources

Brook trout are brilliantly colored with green bodies, yellow and red spots and cream-colored bellies. In the fall the bellies darken to a fiery orange color. The fins of the brook trout are tipped in White. The most distinguishing characteristic of brook trout are the lighter colored worm like markings on their backs.

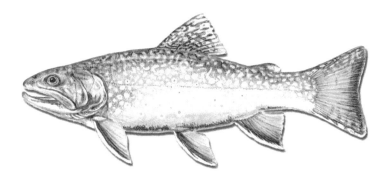

Lake trout in Utah can grow to mammoth proportions with fish topping fifty pounds caught every year. These fish have a gray-brown background overlaid with light spots. Larger lake trout have fewer spots and are very silvery in color. The tail is deeply forked and the mouth matches the size of this fish -- large. Both jaws are imbedded with many strong teeth.

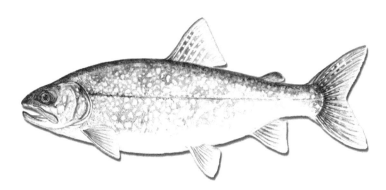

Tiger trout are the brainchild of fishery biologists who have successfully crossed Brown trout and Brook trout to form a new

21

subspecies. Tiger Trout have a unique, dark maze-like pattern over a brownish, gray body. The belly is yellowish orange as are the pectoral, pelvic and anal fins. The tail fin is square like a *brook trout.*

*Fish illustration courtesy of the Utah Department of Wildlife Resources

Splake are another hybrid fish from the DWR labs and is a cross between a Lake Trout and a Brook Trout. It has a dark background with white spots. The tail is not as deeply forked as a lake trout and the pectoral fins are dark with white spots.

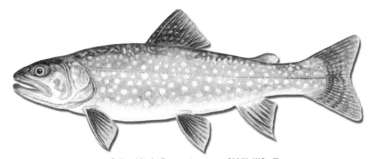

*Fish illustration courtesy of the Utah Department of Wildlife Resources

Arctic Grayling are the sailfish of high mountain lakes. These fish are popular amongst anglers because of their long, high, brilliantly colored, bright purple sail-like fin. Grayling are silvery to light purple on their sides and bluish-white on their bellies. These fish are relatively slender and have a forked tail.

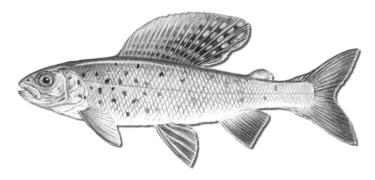

*Fish illustration courtesy of the Utah Department of Wildlife Resources

Kokanee Salmon are landlocked Salmon similar to Sockeyes. Kokanees have a dark blue back with silvery sides. During the fall spawning season they turn a deep red and the lower jaw of the male develops a characteristic hook characteristic of Pacific Salmon. The tail is deeply forked. Kokanee were first introduced to Utah in 1922.

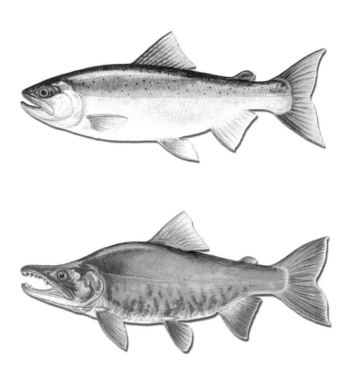

NATIVE GAME FISH

Cutthroat trout are not the only game fish native to Utah. Several other species have evolved in this state's lakes and rivers over millions of years. These fish may not be as glamorous or as sought after as the cutthroat but they do have their supporters. Who said Whitefish can't jump!

Mountain Whitefish can provide winter stream anglers with fast action during their spawning season. These fish are light brown on the back and fins and are white to silvery on the sides and belly. Mountain whitefish have a short and blunt snout and lower jaw with a flap over each nostril.

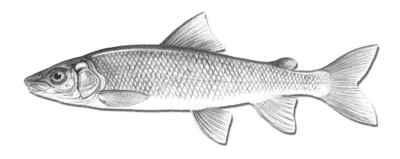

*Fish illustration courtesy of the Utah Department of Wildlife Resources

Bear Lake Whitefish and Bonneville Whitefish are unique species of fish, which only live in Bear Lake and nowhere else in the world. Mature specimens of these two species are indistinguishable. The Bonneville whitefish have gray-blue spots along their sides until they reach about ten inches. Both of these whitefish are elongated in shape and are silvery-white along their sides grading into charcoal gray to black on their backs.

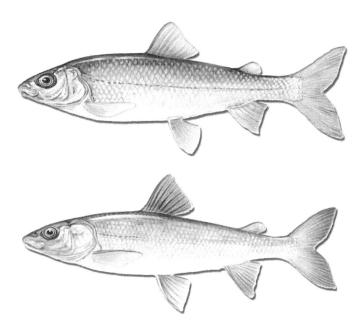

Bonneville Cisco like the Bear Lake and Bonneville Whitefish, are only found in Bear Lake. These fish are long and slender and rarely grow beyond seven inches. They have a dusty blue back and a brassy band along their flanks during the spawn. The snout is sharply pointed. Bonneville Cisco spawns along a rocky beach on the east side of Bear Lake in Mid January.

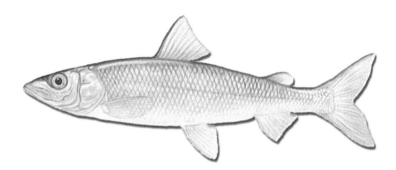

*Fish illustration courtesy of the Utah Department of Wildlife Resources

WARM WATER GAMEFISH

Rod bending Walleye, Largemouth Bass with bucket size mouths, Catfish in Utah! Surprised? Many Utah anglers are unaware of the excellent opportunities Utah offers to catch warm water fish species. For many years the sign of a walleye, perch, bass or any other warm water species in a Utah lake sent fear through the ranks of trout fishermen and the Department of Wildlife Resources. However, over time as more people have moved into this state, attitudes have changed. Many lakes, which were marginal for trout have become excellent warm water fisheries.

Lake Powell is famous for very large striped bass, Starvation Reservoir provides excellent walleye fishing, Willard Bay is home to voracious Wipers and Utah Lake has all the ingredients for huge catfish

Walleyes are the "coyotes" of freshwater. These fish have prominent "canine" teeth, which they can use very effectively to pray on other fish inflict a little revenge on the careless angler. Walleyes look similar to their smaller family member the Yellow Perch. Their coloration ranges from a brassy, olive buff back to yellowish sides and a white belly.

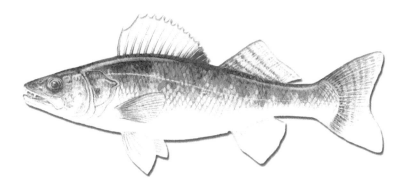

*Fish illustration courtesy of the Utah Department of Wildlife Resources

Smallmouth Bass have just that, smaller mouths then their cousin the Largemouth Bass. They also have a bluntly pointed snout and the lower jaw is slightly longer than the upper jaw. Smallmouth Bass vary in color with habitat, but are generally brown on the back with yellowish sides and bellies. They also have 8 to 15 vertical bars on their sides.

Largemouth Bass are affectionately known to many anglers as bucket mouths because of the extremely large mouth. Largemouth Bass have a very large head and a long mouth which reaches past the center of the eye. The upper parts of the body are greenish with a silvery or brassy luster. The belly is generally white but can also be yellow. There is an irregular dark strip along both sides of the fish.

*Fish illustration courtesy of the Utah Department of Wildlife Resources

Striped Bass are bluish-black to dark gray, the sides are silvery and their bellies are white. Striped Bass have seven to nine unbroken stripes along each side of the body which enhance the streamlined body. These fish grow to impressive sizes and put up an exciting fight.

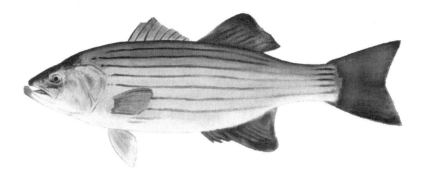

White Bass have similar coloration as Striped Bass with five to seven longitudinal stripes on each side. The body of a White Bass is deeper and less streamlined than the striper.

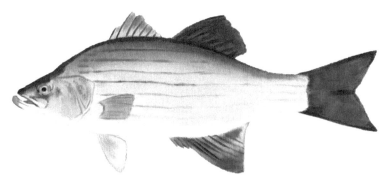

*Fish illustration courtesy of the Utah Department of Wildlife Resources

Yellow perch are a smaller version of the Walleye with more coloration. Yellow Perch have a dark green or black back and yellow sides interspersed with irregular dark spots. Their bellies are white and have seven dark vertical stripes.

*Fish illustration courtesy of the Utah Department of Wildlife Resources

Bluegill are shorter, deep-bodied fish, whose name comes from the dark flap over the gills. The body is olive-green with vertical bars, and some blue and orange may be present.

*Fish illustration courtesy of the Utah Department of Wildlife Resources

Black Crappie are not really black but rather silvery-olive with black and green splotches on the sides and the belly is generally white. Vertical bars are prominent in the young but not in the adults.

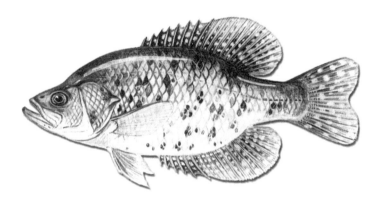

*Fish illustration courtesy of the Utah Department of Wildlife Resources

Green Sunfish are brassy-green or blue-green on the back, sometimes with metallic green flecks and dusky bars on the sides. The flap over the gills is a dark color. This fish will strike at worms, bait or smaller artificial lures.

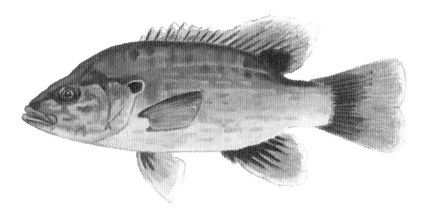

Black Bullhead Catfish will win no beauty contests in the near future. Adults are blackish, dark olive, or dark brown on the back with greenish white or bright yellow bellies.

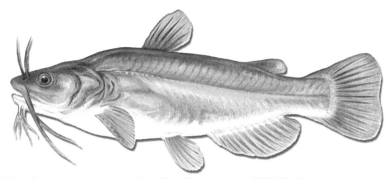

*Fish illustration courtesy of the Utah Department of Wildlife Resources

Channel Catfish are distinguished from other catfishes by their long anal fin and deeply forked tail. The body is a pale bluish-olive on top and bluish-white on the bottom. The sides are covered with spots, which fade with age.

*Fish illustration courtesy of the Utah Department of Wildlife Resources

Common Carp Often considered a trash fish by Utah anglers. Carp have a thick body with gray to brassy green or yellowish green coloration. The body is normally covered with large scales, and carp have fleshy barbells on each side of the mouth. A large spine is present at the front of the dorsal (top) fin. Carp will give you a good fight, grow to a large size, and in some parts of the world is considered a delicacy..

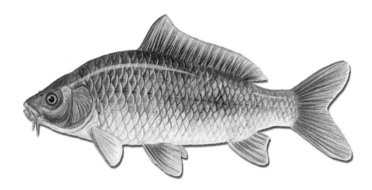

Tiger Muskellunge is a hybrid cross between a Muskellunge and a Northern Pike. These fish have a long torpedo shaped body tipped with a mouth full of very large and sharp teeth. The sides are covered with gray-green vertical bars. The Tiger Muskie can grow to 45 inches in length and weigh well over 20 pounds.

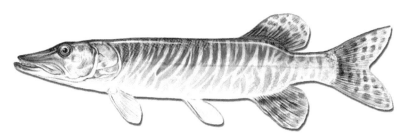

*Fish illustration courtesy of the Utah Department of Wildlife Resources

Great Northern Pike are most often olive green, shading from yellow to white along the belly. The flank is marked with short, light bar-like spots and there are a few too many dark spots on the fins. Sometimes the fins are reddish. Younger Pike have yellow stripes along a green body, later the stripes divide into light spots and the body turns from green to olive green.

*Fish illustration courtesy of the Utah Department of Wildlife Resources

Burbot looks like a lingcod. The Burbot has a serpentine-like body, but it is easily distinguished by a single barbell on the chin. The body is elongated and laterally compressed, with a flattened head and single tube-like projection for each nostril. The mouth is wide, with both upper and lower jaws consisting of many small teeth.

Fish illustration courtesy of the Utah Department of Wildlife Resources

Wipers have the look of a White Bass but have the voracious appetites of the Striped Bass. Wipers are a hybrid cross between a female striped bass and a male white bass and have six to eight dark horizontal stripes over a silvery-white background. Wipers can grow to 24 inches in length and weigh over 12 pounds.

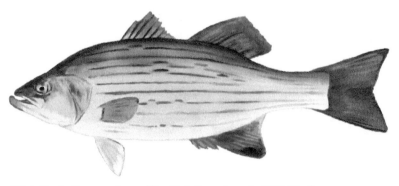

*Fish illustration courtesy of the Utah Department of Wildlife Resources

34

CHAPTER 2

COMMON WILDLIFE OF THE WASATCH MOUNTAINS

There is a lot more to these mountains than just skiing!

The Wasatch Mountain Range is a very robust and diverse ecosystem and more than 300 species of animals call these mountains home. Many people live their whole lives near these majestic mountains without realizing how close they are to wilderness of this quality and expansiveness. Three large federally designated wilderness areas are located in the Wasatch Mountains located next to Salt Lake City. These protected areas are the 11,500 acre Twin Peaks Wilderness area, the 30,100 acre Lone Peak Wilderness area and the 15,300 acre Mount Olympus Wilderness area. There are also hundreds of thousands of acres of prime mountain habitat located in the Wasatch Cache and Uinta National Forest located adjacent to Utah's most populated metropolitan areas. Almost all of this is public ground and is set aside and protected for all of the citizens of Utah and the nation.

The area of the Wasatch Mountains covered in this book has literally become an island of wilderness surrounded by major highways, cities and towns on all sides. This treasure will continue to have its borders populated by more people and all of the impacts associated with population growth. Because of this reality, we all need to be as attentive, protective and proactive as past generations to protect this precious resource.

The following is a list of the most common animals that you might encounter when you are hiking to the lakes in the Wasatch. Remember that these animals are wild and can be dangerous. If you see or come into contact with any of these animals give them the proper space they are due. Never harass, chase or stress any of animals that you come upon but rather be quiet and enjoy watching them in their natural habitat. Remember you are a guest in their house.

Mule deer are common state-wide in Utah and can be found in many types of habitat, ranging from open deserts to high mountains and as their habitat shrinks, in urban areas as well. Mule Deer are commonly seen along the trails in the Wasatch Mountains. In the spring, the does are often seen with yearling fawns. During the Bow hunt in late August, these animals will become more wary as they are pursued by hunters.

Elk are common in most mountainous regions of Utah including the Wasatch Mountains where they can be found in mountain meadows and forests during the summer and in foothills and valley grasslands during the winter. Elk may be active during both day and night, but most activity occurs around dusk and again at dawn. Look for these majestic animals when hiking to these lakes. During the heat of the day, the elk will retreat to the deep, dark pines to bed down. Even though these animals can weigh more than 1000 pounds, they can still be difficult to see in these stands of pines.

Females (cows) typically give birth to their calves in the late spring. Look for cow elk and their calves grazing in grassy meadows.

When hiking to the lakes in the fall, listen for the haunting bugle sounds from the bulls looking for a mate!

Moose In Utah, this large ungulate species can be found in the mountains of the northern and northeastern portion of the state. Moose prefer forest habitats, especially locations with a mixture of wooded areas and open areas near lakes or wetlands and there is a stable and growing population in the Wasatch Mountains.

Moose breed in the late summer or early fall, and females typically give birth to one (rarely two) calves in late spring. Moose are herbivores that prefer to feed on aquatic vegetation and new woody growth during the spring and summer. It is possible to see moose at nearly ever lake in the forested and meadow zones of the Wasatch. They also can be seen near marshy areas of streams or where beaver ponds are located. Be careful when you encounter a moose, especially one with a calf. Every year Moose kill more people in the United States than bears so don't ever crowd a moose and never get between a mother Moose and her calf.

*Wildlife Photography courtesy of the Utah Department of Wildlife Resources

Mountain Goats prefer extremely steep and rugged areas above the timberline, and are excellent rock climbers. They typically migrate to lower elevations in the winter. Sometimes you can spot these animals when you are fishing at the highest elevation lakes. I have seen Mountain Goats above Upper Red Pine Lake, White Pine Lake, Upper Bells Reservoir Silver Lake and Silver Glance Lake in American Fork Canyon. It is possible to see them at other high elevation lakes as well. Look for little white dots on the cliffs above the lakes.

38

Black Bear are fairly common in Utah and are found primarily in large forested areas and are present throughout the Wasatch Mountains. The Black Bear is not always black and can vary in color from reddish to light brown to black. I recently saw a Black Bear during an early spring fishing trip above Silver Lake in American Fork Canyon. The bear must have just come out of hibernation and was traversing the high snow fields above the lake looking for food.

Black Bears are omnivores with diets consisting of fruits, insects, grubs, some small vertebrates, and carrion. They breed in June or July, and young are born in January or February. Black Bears are nocturnal and are dormant during the winter. It is a very rare treat to see one of these creatures when hiking to a lake.

Bears are a great symbol of wilderness in the Wasatch but have (very) rarely been known to attack. It is important to practice safe bear precautions when hiking, fishing and especially camping in the Wasatch Mountains.

*Wildlife Photography courtesy of the Utah Department of Wildlife Resources

Mountain Lions can be found throughout Utah, but are rarely seen due to their secretive nature. I have never seen a Mountain Lion while fishing in the Wasatch but I suspect maybe a couple have seen me! These are beautiful and majestic animals and if you do see one in the wild it is a rare and special treat. Females produce one litter of one to six kittens about every two years. Cougars are active year-round, during both day and night, although most activity occurs at dawn and dusk. Cougars are carnivores, with diets composed of deer, rabbits, rodents, and other animals. Of course if you ever do encounter a Mountain Lion in the wild, exercise common sense and keep your distance.

Bobcats are common throughout Utah, although like mountain lions they are a rarely seen and very secretive species. Bobcats prefer areas with thick undergrowth, and can be found in deserts, mountains, and numerous other types of habitat. They are primarily active at night and seek shelter in rocks, trees, or hollow logs when inactive. Bobcats are typically solitary except when breeding.

Coyotes are common in Utah and in the Wasatch Mountains. While heavily hunted, these animals are successful breeders and will produce one litter of four to seven pups during the spring. Coyotes can be heard howling and barking in the early morning hours and at dusk. If camping at one of the lakes you may hear these song dogs serenade you at night.

Red Fox are common in Utah, where they are primarily found in open and semi-open habitats, although occasionally in forested areas, cities, and suburban settings. I have been lucky to see these animals while hiking to several lakes. Red fox are not always red, but can be any shade between red and black. The red fox can be distinguished from other fox species by the characteristic white tip on the end of the tail.

Beaver are very common in Utah and are found in the Wasatch Mountains. They prefer permanent slow moving streams, ponds, small lakes, and reservoirs. Beaver are mainly nocturnal but are occasionally seen during the day. They do not hibernate but usually become less active during the winter.

Beavers cut trees to build dams and water diversions, sometimes creating large ponds. Lodges of sticks and mud are often constructed near these ponds and are used by beaver families for shelter, food storage, and the rearing of their young. These ponds are also great locations for fish and are excellent to target when fishing in the Wasatch. Anglers owe the beaver a great debt of gratitude for the ponds created by their damns.

*Wildlife Photography courtesy of the Utah Department of Wildlife Resources

Skunks are found throughout the Wasatch Range. They are nocturnal but can be sometimes be seen during the day when hiking to the lakes. Often, their distinctive and unpleasant odor will alert you to their presence. Look for skunks around meadows and marshy areas. Be careful around skunks not only because they can spray you with their awful scent but they occasionally can be carriers of the rabies virus.

Snowshoe Hare can reach 14 inches in length and weigh up to four pounds, with ears three to four inches long. There is a stable population of these hares in the Wasatch. In summer, the upper parts are dark brown and the under parts, behind the front legs, whitish. The tail is brownish on top and dusky beneath. In winter, its pelage is all white with a black eye ring.

In Utah, this species is limited to coniferous forests, interspersed with thickets of aspen, willow, and alder in the higher mountainous areas.

Yellow-bellied marmots are large (five to ten pound) rodents that exist in large numbers throughout the Wasatch Range. Yellow-bellied marmots prefer meadows near forested areas. They dig burrows under rocks and logs, and retreat to those burrows to hibernate during the cold winter months.

*Wildlife Photography courtesy of the Utah Department of Wildlife Resources

Pika can be found in only a few of the high mountain ranges of Utah where it prefers areas above the tree line on rocky slopes. Pikas are found in the Wasatch Range and are active during the day throughout the year, but may remain under cover during hot days. I have seen these little creatures only near the lakes at the highest elevations.

*Wildlife Photography courtesy of the Utah Department of Wildlife Resources

Golden Eagles are quite common in Utah.

Typically this eagle is found in open country, especially in mountainous regions. It feeds mainly on small mammals, especially rabbits, marmots, and ground squirrels. I have seen these eagles soaring in the wind currents above many of the high lakes.

*All Wildlife Photography courtesy of the Utah Department of Wildlife Resources

46

CHAPTER 3
NECESSARY TOOLS OF THE TRADE
KNOWLEDGE CAN BE A GOOD THING!

The equipment you will need for a successful trip.

What are the fish hitting? This question echo's through the Wasatch canyons and peaks every day because the fish of these mountains can have picky appetites; or they can reward the lucky with fast paced action. If you have fished alpine lakes and small streams you have most likely experienced this reality.

Fishing the Alpine lakes, reservoirs and streams of the Wasatch is really no different from fishing any other body of water full of hungry pan sized trout. Over the years, I have come to rely on certain flies, lures and techniques that consistently provide fast action when the bite is on and produce strikes when the fishing is slow. By no means are the patterns and techniques discussed in this chapter the only patterns and techniques that will work on these waters. However, I do highly recommend that at least some of these flies and lures be in your vest to increase the chance of a successful fishing trip.

If you are like me, you have many boxes of flies, lures and jigs. Every time I prepare to hike to a favorite lake I swear I will only bring one tackle box and every time the backpack somehow fills up with several boxes. In the back of all fishermen's minds lurks the fear that they will be caught on a lake or stream during an incredible bite only to find out they didn't bring the right "box"! Fortunately for everyone, when fishing in the Wasatch, it is not necessary to bring your entire arsenal. The success of many patterns is determined by the time of year that you are fishing. The following is a guide to those successful patterns and techniques.

47

RESERVOIRS AND ALPINE LAKES

JIG FISHING

To some, Jig fishing is not as glamorous as fly-fishing, lure fishing and in some minds even bait fishing and therefore is not practiced as extensively as it is in other states. This is unfortunate since jig fishing can be very successful, especially early in the season when the ice is just melting. On a recent spring trip to the Lake Blanche Basin, My buddy and I caught over 100 brook trout on small white and red mini-tube jigs as well as small emerger patterns, yet we could not get a strike on any metal lure or any other fly patterns. In fact, we had similar experiences on most of the high alpine lakes covered in this book. One of the most successful methods to entice Brook Trout is to fish with a 1/16 ounce mini-tube jig. This is especially true when the fish are cruising the shorelines in search of food after their long winter under the ice. Almost every cast is met with a hard strike, and if it's a big one, a reel screaming run to the deepest sections of the lake.

Color seems to play an important role on these waters. White and red are the best producing colors year round. A good rule of thumb when choosing which color jig to tie on is to look to the sky. If the sky is overcast use darker colors and as the sky brightens move towards lighter colored jigs. Sometimes certain colors will quickly turn hot then cold, so be willing to switch off to something different.

When jig fishing, it is important to have a light, flexible rod. Graphite rods work well but ultra light glass rods work best. Kencor makes an excellent glass rod; however, they are hard to find in Utah. Kencor recently filed bankruptcy and it may be necessary to go online to find one. An ultra light glass rod will outperform even the lightest and most advanced graphite rods. Graphite tends to be too stiff to get the proper swimming action on the jig. We also recommend that you outfit your rod with an ultra light-spinning reel. There are many reels on the market to choose from and we suggest that you don't pinch pennies on this important piece of gear. There is nothing more frustrating than to hike to the top of the world and have your reel malfunction. Fill your reel with 4 pound clear or glacial colored line, especially since these lakes are fed by snow melt.

Technique is important when fishing with a jig. It is crucial to present the jig properly. Cast your jig near structure or a drop off and let it sink for a few seconds before beginning your retrieve. Hold your rod at a 45-degree angle out in front of you and twitch up and down while at the same time taking up the slack created by the twitching. This will draw the jig constantly towards you. Vary the twitching, depth and retrieval speed until you connect. Many times the fish will strike on the downward motion of the jig so be prepared to snap back and set the hook.

If you have fished with a jig, you know that there are hundreds of colors, sizes and styles to choose from. Our experience dictates that mini-tube jigs in 1/32 and 1/16 ounce consistently outperform all other jig styles and weights. The most effective colors have been solid white, red with white legs, smoke or pink colors with black specks, yellow and green with rainbow colored specks. I caught a five pound cutthroat on Upper Red Pine Lake on the latter color jig.

SPINNERS AND LURES

Fishing with lures and spinners ("metal") can be successful, especially during warm summer afternoons. Fishing with metal allows the angler opportunity to cover more water and reach greater depths from the shore.

49

On one unusually warm summer day on a trip to Silver Lake in Big Cottonwood Canyon, the water was calm, the sky a brilliant blue and the temperature was hovering in the eighties, with no surface activity on the lake. Several anglers were trying their luck with worms and power bait but were having no success. As I approached the lake, I ruled out dry flies and decided to tie on a gold Lil-Jake with red spots. My casts broke the perfect calm of the lake, as did the fish when they hit these lures with a vengeance. Cast after cast brought in pan sized Brookies and Rainbows. It wasn't long before the heat of the day was broken by the chilly stares of my bait-dunking neighbors. I have had similar experiences on Silver Flat Reservoir, Tibble Fork Reservoir, Pittsburgh Lake and White Pine Lake. All of these lakes produce well in the summer for anglers willing to use metal and get to where the fish are.

Overall, the best success has been with Lil-Jakes in gold with red spots, silver with red spots, black with yellow or green spots and white with red or black spots. Gold is probably the best all around color and produces fish when the others don't. Spinners such as Mepps in orange, green, gold or silver also work well. Rooster tails in gold or silver with a red or orange skirt will also produce. Pot o' Gold's and daredevils in red and white, silver or gold will also help you toward your limit of trout.

As with jig fishing, technique is important when presenting your lure to the trout. The secret is to take a systematic approach to fishing with metal. Before making that first cast, try to imagine a 180' semi-circle in front of you on the water. Begin casting from one side of the circle, making sure to cover all water systematically until you finish on the other side then reverse direction and repeat. It is important to allow your lure to sink a little deeper each time you cover the circle. This allows you to cover all water depths within your semi-circle.

50

For example, with the first set of casts allow your lure to sink for one second before you begin your retrieve. For your second set of casts allow 2 seconds before beginning you retrieve. For your third set of casts allow 3 seconds and so on. Continue until you have found the depth where the fish are holding or until you hit bottom. Thoroughly cover your area and all depths before you move to the next spot. If you do this you will catch more fish.

FLY FISHING

It seems that everyone today is a fly fisherman! The sport has exploded in popularity with thousands of new recruits every year casting their lines into rivers and lakes all over this great country of ours. Gone are the days when you could sneak out of work early on a warm summer day, head up to one of the local canyon streams with fly rod in hand and be the only fly fisherman fishing the good holes. Now, especially on weekends you are lucky to find a spot. Solitude can still be found but you must be willing to hike. The alpine lakes of the Wasatch are truly undiscovered by fly fisherman.

While preparing for the writing of this book, I hiked to all the lakes and only saw one other fly fisherman. The only explanation for this apparent lack of use is ignorance. Everyone knows about the great fly fishing on the Provo River, Green River, Weber River, Strawberry River and Strawberry Reservoir but few know of the opportunities to catch 5 to 10 pound cutthroats in their own backyards.

Fly fishing these lakes is rewarding but challenging. The biggest challenge will be the wind. Mountains produce their own weather and the Wasatch has a fondness for wind.

The wind is a constant on many of these lakes and makes it difficult to cast. To combat the wind, use a heavy rod in a 5 or

51

6 weight. One of the benefits of the wind is that it will blow terrestrials into the water and bring the fish closer to shore. Many of these lakes also have very little room for back casts. It is important that you are proficient with your roll casts to avoid spending most of your day in the trees.

One of the greatest times spent fly fishing in the Wasatch was on Pittsburgh Lake. This little lake is tucked high into a cirque below the backside of snowbird and is full of 8 to 14 inch brookies. There are so many fish in this lake that when they rise it looks as if it is raining on the water. Even with all these fish, this lake is still a challenge. The reason, it is ringed with heavy timber on the east, west, and south and the north side of the lake is steep and covered with large boulders. However, patience combined with proper casting techniques will provide you with an unforgettable experience. This is true on almost all of these lakes with the exception of a few above timberline that have a little more space to cast.

Summer and fall are the best times to fly fish on these lakes. During spring, the water is still pretty cold and the bug life not as active. In spring you can have success with midge patterns as well as emergers. Streamers also work well in the spring, especially just after ice off. Brown, black, red and purple Wooly Buggers, Damsel fly nymphs and leaches work especially well. During summer, you will experience the many aquatic hatches that take place on these lakes. Mosquitoes, Caddis, and mayflies make up a large portion of the trout's diet with terrestrial rounding out their menu. The best dry fly patterns for these lakes have been Mosquitoes, Elk Hair Caddis, Blue Wing Olives, Royal Wulffs, and Renegades in a size 16 – 20. As mentioned earlier, the wind is a constant and because of that wind many terrestrials end up on the water. The best terrestrial patterns have been Dave's Hoppers, Parachute Hoppers, Beetle imitations, black and red ants, and Chernobyl Ants. It is important that you match the size and color of your terrestrial patterns as close to the ones floating on the lake as possible. During the fall, the fish are in a feeding frenzy eating almost anything that lands on the water.

Attractor patterns such as Royal Wulffs and Renegades work well during the fall as do Wooly Buggers and leach patterns.

Nymphs work well during spring, summer and fall, especially when there is no activity on the surface. Pheasant tails, Prince Nymphs, Hares ears, Zug bugs, Brassies and small egg patterns in orange and yellow are all effective. When fishing nymphs or streamers an intermediate to full sinking line can be helpful on these lakes.

The following is a breakdown of our recommendations for artificial flies, lures, jigs and necessary equipment for use on the waters of the Wasatch Range.

ARTIFICAL LURES:

Jigs: 1/32 and 1/16 size jigs work well. Jigs are most effective on lakes just after ice off since the fish are closer to shore. Jigs are effective most anytime on streams. The most effective colors have been solid white, red with white legs, smoke colored with black specks, pink with black specks, and yellow. Mini-tube jigs are the most productive style of jig. Grub jigs do not seem to be as effective as the mini-tube jigs.

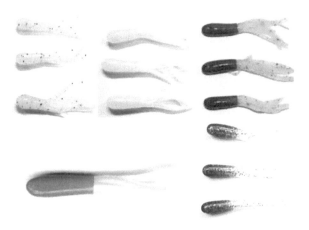

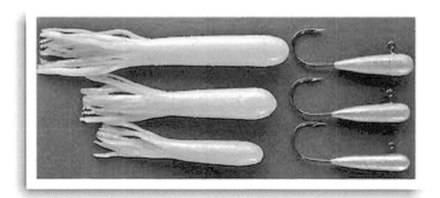

Lures: The most productive lure throughout the Wasatch would have to be Lil Jake's in 0's and 1's. The best colors are Gold with red spots, silver with red spots, and black with yellow spots. Crocodiles and Dare Devils in rainbow or gold also produce fish. Vibrax Lures work well in the streams.

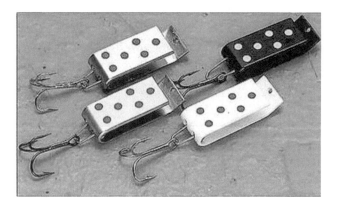

Lil Jakes

Crocodiles

Dare Devil

Spinners: #1 Mepps spinners and Rooster tails work well; also any other small or medium spinner in silver or gold may produce fish.

 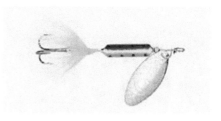

Mepps   **Rooster tail**

Rods: Light weight spinning rods, jig rods

Line: light pound test up to 6 pound.

FLY FISHING:

Streamers - Brown, Black and purple Woolly Buggers, Damsel Fly nymphs and Egg Sucking Leaches in sizes 8 through 12.

Damsel Fly

Woolly Bugger   **Egg Sucking Leach**

Nymphs - Bead Head Prince Nymphs, Beadhead and regular Hares ears, pheasant tails, Zug Bugs, Brassies and small egg patterns in orange and yellow are all effective.

Hares Ear

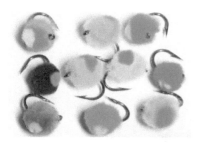

Egg Pattens   **Pheasant Tail**

Zug Bug   **Bead Head Prince Nymph**

Emergers - Serendipities and Timberline Emergers.

Timberline Emerger   **Serendipities**

Dry Flies - Midges, Mosquitoes, Renegades, Royal Wulffs, Beetles, Grasshoppers, and ants all work well. Sizes will vary with each fly. For the terrestrials try using Dave's Hoppers, Parachute Hoppers, Crowe Beetles or any other beetle imitation, Black Ant imitations and Chernobyl Ants. Attractor patterns like Renegades and Royal Wulffs work well in sizes 12 through 18.

Rods: Fly rods in 3, 4, 5 and 6 weight.

Line types: Floating line on all lakes and streams. Sinking lines work well at White Pine Lake, Twin Lakes and Upper Bells Reservoir.

CHAPTER 4
STREAMS AND CREEKS

BIG COTTONWOOD CREEK, LITTLE COTTONWOOD
CREEK, MILL CREEK, PARLEY'S CREEK, CITY CREEK,
LITTLE DELL CREEK, AMERICAN FORK CREEK

STREAMS AND CREEKS

Fishing the streams and creeks of the Wasatch has to be one of my favorite past times. These streams tumble down from the high alpine lakes clear, cold and full of trout. They might not be famous tail water fisheries but these streams provide the urban angler with the necessary respite from both the heat and congestion of the valley below. On Weekends you will find many fishermen on the more popular streams such as Big Cottonwood and Millcreek. However, there are many more creeks and streams where the pressure is light and the fishing superb.

Many of these hidden and not so hidden waters require light line, short rods and the prowess of a mountain lion. Some of the smaller creeks are only as wide as a kitchen table and are covered by a thick canopy of trees and shrubs requiring the angler to get on all fours to reach some good holes. Since these creeks require a little more effort to fish, and are unknown to many anglers, the fish tend to be larger and easier to catch.

When fishing on these waters I usually prefer to fish with a fly. However, lures, spinners and jigs are very effective on all the small streams and creeks in the Wasatch. If you plan to fish with any of these you will want to use a light graphite rod with ultra light spinning gear. If you plan to use a jig we recommend you stick with a glass rod for better presentation of the jig. All of the patterns, which work on the lakes, will produce fish on these streams and creeks.

FLY FISHING

Accessibility is the only major obstacle facing the stream angler. With over 500 inches of snow a year these small streams and even smaller creeks fill to flood stage in spring and stay high and muddy well into summer. On average snow years, the bigger streams are not fish-able until July with heavy snow years delaying fishing until August. A few fishermen try their luck while the rivers are roaring in the small back eddies and behind large boulders that are less affected by the heavy flows. I do not recommend you try this. It is

62

true that you might catch a few fish but you might also drown in the process. It's best to wait until the water recedes to normal levels.

Once the water is safe to wade, the streams provide fast action for Brown, Cutthroat, Brook and Rainbow Trout. There is no more exciting way to catch these fish then on a dry fly. A favorite pattern would have to be the Royal Wulff in a size 14 – 18. I prefer this fly for two good reasons: One, it is easy to see and two, it simply catches more fish on these streams than any other pattern.

The best way to fish these waters is to work the deep holes, bends in the stream, under willows and trees and near small waterfalls. Beaver ponds provide great habitat for fish and should be worked thoroughly. Big Cottonwood Creek has several areas where beavers have crafted homes, and every year I catch several large browns and brook trout out of these small ponds. The best beaver ponds are the ones that are situated on sections of streams, which are not readily accessible from a road. The larger beaver ponds attract more fishermen and are usually hit harder. Dry fly action on beaver ponds can be fast and furious.

Summer and fall are the best times to fish these streams. Begin your fishing season by concentrating on the lakes in early spring when they are just beginning to ice off. This will keep you busy from late April to early July. In July switch your emphasis from the high lake's to the lower streams which are just beginning to clear up and become fish-able. Try to target your fishing during the middle of the week to avoid the crowded conditions on the weekends. It is possible to have any of the streams in the Wasatch to yourself if you are able to fish during the week. The canyons have a whole different feel and appearance during the week and the fishing is a whole lot better.

During the summer, terrestrial patterns are very effective on these streams. Parachute Hoppers, beetles and ant patterns are deadly. Fish these patterns near stream side grasses or overhanging willows. To successfully fish these two types of cover, cast onto the grasses and allow the drag to pull your fly into the water and drift naturally along the streams' edge. For overhanging willows, cast above the willow and let your fly drift underneath. Both of these techniques will entice lightning fast strikes so be prepared to set the hook. Once you have seen a trout rise to a terrestrial pattern you will never want to fish with a tiny midge again. The sheer power and beauty of the strike is hard to explain and has to be seen to be appreciated.

Fall fly-fishing is spectacular and so is the scenery. Sometime in early September when the first cold night heralds the arrival of fall the fish instinctively know that the feeding bonanza is about to end and long cold winter days lay ahead. This is the time that just about anything you throw on the water will be intercepted by a pair of fish lips. Many of the streams contain good populations of brown trout. In these streams food is not the only thing on the brown trout's mind. Fall is a romantic time for the brown and spawning is in full swing. During the spawn these fish are not always thinking of eating, to entice these spawning trout it may be necessary to cast a streamer or egg pattern in front of their noses in order to irate them into striking. Please remember to watch where you are stepping to avoid stepping in the Redds. Redds are the nests where the fish have laid hundreds of eggs. One careless fisherman can kill thousands of fish in a single day.

Look for lighter colored areas in the stream where it is evident that a fish has disturbed the gravel and then steer clear.

The following are the fish species you are likely to catch by stream;

Big Cottonwood Creek

Brook Trout

Rainbow Trout

Brown Trout

Cutthroat Trout

64

Little Cottonwood Creek

Cutthroat Trout

Brown Trout

Rainbow Trout

Mill Creek

Cutthroat Trout

City Creek

Cutthroat Trout

Parley's Creek

Cutthroat Trout

American Fork Creek

Rainbow Trout

Brown Trout

Cutthroat Trout

Little Dell Creek

Cutthroat Trout

CHAPTER 5

WATERSHED AND WILDERNESS RESTRICTIONS

Photo by Tony Nelson

WATERSHED

The Wasatch Mountains and the waters that flow down from them are the main water supply for 60 percent of the Wasatch Front. Think of it this way, if you live within the Wasatch front, six out of every ten glasses of water out of your tap has its beginnings as rain or snow high up in the Wasatch Range. The Wasatch Mountains are popular for hiking, fishing, hunting, wildlife viewing, mountain biking,

66

snowmobiling, snow shoeing, rock climbing and many other activities. Hundreds of thousands of people visit, recreate, wade and utilize your drinking water well before it ever reaches your tap. The excessive usage of these mountains would have a negative impact on the quality of the water if it was not for very strict government rules and regulations.

Most of the lakes and streams covered in this book fall within the Salt Lake Watershed and are regulated by the Salt Lake City Water Department, Salt Lake County Health Department, Salt Lake County Sheriff's Department and the United States Forest Service Salt Lake District Office.

Most people do not realize that it is a privilege and not a right to fish in the streams and lakes of the Wasatch Mountains. The main purpose for this water is for the usage of the citizens along the Wasatch Front. As fishermen, we need to be extra vigilant when plying our sport on the lakes and streams of the Wasatch. We have hiked to many a lake where careless fisherman have left trash, empty soda or beer cans, plastic water bottles, monofilament fishing line, cigarette butts and various sorts of other trash behind. This is wrong and will eventually lead to restrictions and limits on where fishing will be allowed if we do not regulate ourselves and fellow fishermen. Fishermen are not the only culprits. Hikers, campers, wildlife viewers, mountain bike enthusiasts, skiers and everyone else that use and enjoy these mountains need to be as vigilant as fishermen to keep the mountains pristine and the waters clean. No one wants to hike to a remote alpine lake and find the place littered with trash, diapers, old bike tires, etc.

Leave no trace! If you see trash, bend over and pick it up and bring it back with you to dispose of properly. Everyone will benefit from your efforts.

Salt Lake Watershed Rules

The following are the rules posted by the Salt Lake Ranger District for camping in the Wasatch Mountains watershed. Salt Lake City Watershed Restrictions apply and are strictly enforced.

Back-country camping is not permitted within 200 ft of any open water (lakes, streams, etc). Pets are not allowed at all (not even in your car!). Swimming is not allowed in lakes or streams. Visitors must carry out everything they bring in, including food scraps and fruit peels. Follow general ""Leave No Trace"" guidelines for disposal of human waste. Pollution of any kind will not be accepted. Watershed regulations are enforced by the Salt Lake County Sheriff's Office, the Salt Lake City Water Department, the Salt Lake City - County Health Department, the US Forest Service, and the Alta Marshal's Office. Violations constitute a Class ""B"" misdemeanor and in most cases a citation is issued to violators.

WASATCH WILDNERESS

In 1978 and again in 1984 Congress permanently protected approximately 37,000 acres of Utah's Wasatch Mountain alpine terrain. Nearly 2 million people live along the Wasatch Front. With this many people living so close to these important mountains it is important that we protect as much of it as possible from development, excessive transportation impacts within the canyons, and overuse by recreationalists, environmentalists and everyone else that loves the natural beauty and wildness of this area.

Lone Peak National Wilderness Area – 30,544 acres. The Lone Peak Wilderness is Utah's first designated Wilderness. It includes 11,253 feet of Lone Peak which looms over the city of Draper in the valley below. There are several lakes that hold good size cutthroats and brook trout within the wilderness boundaries.

Mt Olympus National Wilderness Area – 15,279 acres. Established by Congress in 1984 along with the Twin Peaks National Wilderness as part of the Utah Wilderness Act, Mt Olympus Wilderness is home for many back country hiking trips. This wilderness contains no lakes with fish in them. Mount Olympus towers over the Salt Lake Valley at 9,026 feet

Twin Peaks National Wilderness Area – 11,447 acres. The Twin Peaks wilderness includes Twin Peak which is 11,319 feet above sea level. This wilderness has many high alpine lakes full of feisty and hungry fish. It is also a great area to watch wildlife.

Lone Peak Wilderness Restrictions

Motorized equipment and equipment used for mechanical transport is generally prohibited on all federal lands designated as wilderness. This includes the use of motor vehicles, motorboats, motorized equipment, bicycles, hang gliders, wagons, carts, portage wheels, and the landing of aircraft including helicopters, unless provided for in specific legislation.

In a few areas some exceptions allowing the use of motorized equipment or mechanical transport are described in the special regulations in effect for a specific area.

The following wilderness regulations are in effect for this area. Not all regulations are in effect for every wilderness.

Campfires:

--Campfires are prohibited year-round at Upper Red Pine and Red Pine Lake in the Lone Peak Wilderness area.

Travel:

--To lessen soil erosion, it is prohibited to shortcut trail switchbacks.

Group Size:

--The maximum group size on the Pleasant Grove Ranger District is 15 people per group.

--The maximum group size on the Salt Lake Ranger District is 10 people per group.

Mount Olympus Wilderness Restrictions

The Mount Olympus Wilderness area is closed to motor vehicles, motorized equipment, hang gliders and bicycles. In addition, parts of this wilderness lay within the culinary watershed for Salt Lake County and special restrictions concerning camping, swimming, and domestic animals apply.

The following acts are prohibited in the Mount Olympus Wilderness Area:

Group sizes exceeding 10 persons for overnight use.

Camping within 200 feet of lakes, trails, or other sources of water.

Camping for a period of 3 days at an individual site.

Short-cutting a trail switchback and disposing of garbage, debris, or other waste.

Twin Peaks Wilderness Restrictions

Motorized equipment and equipment used for mechanical transport is generally prohibited on all federal lands designated as wilderness. This includes the use of motor vehicles, motorboats, motorized equipment, bicycles, hang gliders, wagons, carts, portage wheels, and the landing of aircraft including helicopters, unless provided for in specific legislation.

In a few areas some exceptions allowing the use of motorized equipment or mechanical transport are described in the special regulations in effect for a specific area.

The following wilderness regulations are in effect for this area. Not all regulations are in effect for every wilderness.

Campfires:

--Campfires are prohibited year-round in the Twin Peaks Wilderness

70

area.

Travel:

--To lessen soil erosion, it is prohibited to shortcut trail switchbacks.

Group Size:

--The maximum group size on the Salt Lake Ranger District is 10 people per group.

For up to date information and for any specific questions contact the following government agencies;

Salt Lake County Health Department, Environmental Health Services

(385) 468-3860
788 East Woodoak Lane (5380 South)
Murray, Utah 84107-6379

Watershed Management
Salt Lake City Department of Public Utilities

1530 S. West Temple
Salt Lake City, Utah 84115
(801) 483-6705

Uinta-Wasatch Cache Salt Lake Ranger District Office

Supervisor's Office
(801) 999-2103
857 West South Jordan Parkway
South Jordan, UT 84095
Mon-Fri:8:00am - 4:30pm

CHAPTER 6
THE LAKES OF

BIG COTTONWOOD

DRAINAGE

LAKE BLANCHE, LAKE FLORENCE, LAKE LILLIAN, SILVER LAKE, TWIN LAKES, LAKE MARY, LAKE MARTHA, DOG LAKE "MILLCREEK DRAINAGE", LAKE DESOLATION, DOG LAKE "BRIGHTON"
LAKE CATHERINE
LAKE BLANCHE, LAKE FLORENCE AND
LAKE LILLIAN

LAKE BLANCHE
LAKE FLORENCE
AND
LAKE LILLIAN

Lake Blanche (Photo Courtesy of Eric Bean)

ELEVATION: 8920 feet above sea level.

ICE OFF: The southern exposure allows these lakes to be one of the first in the high country to shed their protective coating of ice. Ice off generally occurs around the latter part of May. However, on years when the snowpack is extremely heavy, access to these lakes may not be possible until the first week in June.

73

FISHING USAGE: Weekdays - light , Weekends - moderate.

HIKING MILES: 2 3/4 miles.

HIKING TIME: 2 1/2 to 3 hours.

AVERAGE SIZE OF FISH: The average size of the fish range from 8 to 12 inches with some reaching 14 inches. The Brook trout in these lakes may not be large fish but what they lack in size they make up for in beauty and fighting skill.

WILDERNESS AREA: Twin Peaks Wilderness Area.

FISH SPECIES PRESENT: Brook Trout

STOCKING SCHEDULE: Trout are stocked by plane every other year. Check with the Utah Division of Wildlife Resources for the stocking schedule for this lake.

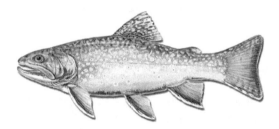

HOW TO GET THERE:

These lakes are located within the "Mill B South Fork Drainage" in Big Cottonwood Canyon. The trail head to Lake Blanche is located 4.5 miles from the mouth of the canyon at the S-Turn. The Forest Service has recently improved the facilities and enlarged the parking area to better accommodate visitors to this popular hiking destination. From the parking area it is necessary to hike along Big Cottonwood Creek for a quarter of a mile to a sign, located on the right, marking the beginning of the trail. The Lake Blanche trail is well maintained and takes you through one of the most beautiful glacial carved canyons in the Wasatch. The Lake Blanche basin with its three lakes consisting of Blanche, Florence and Lillian is a result of this glacial ice. The power of these glaciers is evidenced in the glass smooth rocks and boulders that surround the lakes in this basin. The trail head begins next to the Mill B South Fork stream that flows out of Lake Lillian. The trail continues along the stream for 1 3/4 miles until you reach an overgrown meadow. This section of the trail is well maintained and the hike is fairly easy and scenic. Once you get to the meadow area the trail veers to the left and ascends several switchbacks through a grove of tall aspens. This section of the trail is approximately 2/3 of a mile long and is well marked but the difficulty of the hike increases. The final section of the trail begins as you emerge out of the aspen grove. This section of the trail is approximately 1/3 of a mile long and ascends a rocky area. It is possible from these rocks to view parts of Salt Lake County and the Great Salt Lake. The vegetation on this part of the trail consists of mosses, lichens and alpine wildflowers. Caution should be observed when hiking on these smooth rock fields especially when they are wet. The trail ends at a deteriorating rock wall overlooking Lake Blanche.

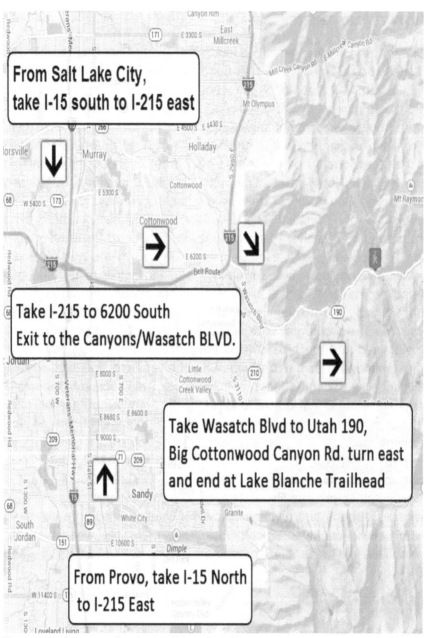

Topography map for Lake Blanche, Florence and Lillian

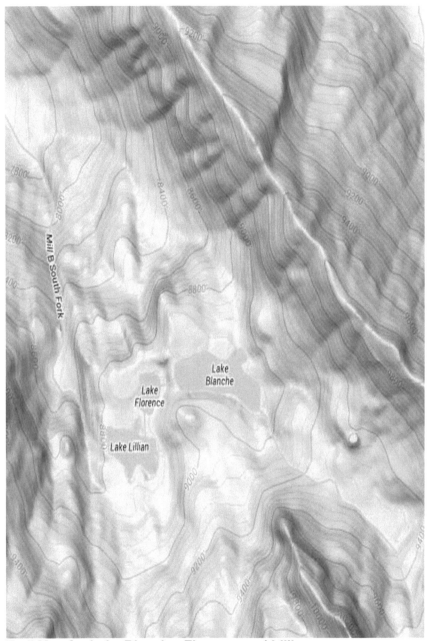

Trail Map for Lake Blanche, Florence and Lillian

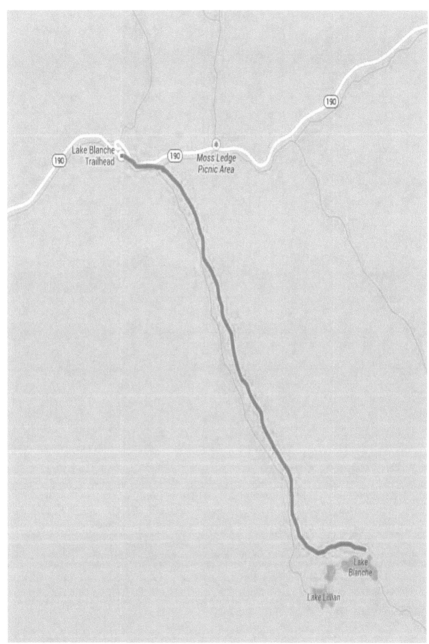

Trail Map for Lake Blanche, Florence and Lillian

Lake Lillian (Photo Courtesy of WasatchHiker.com)

Lake Florence (Photo Courtesy of WasatchHiker.com)

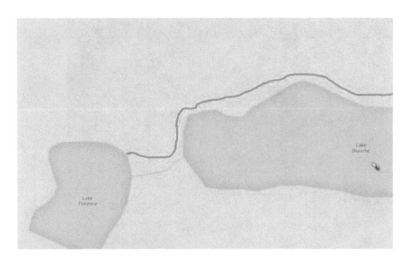

Lake Florence Trail Map

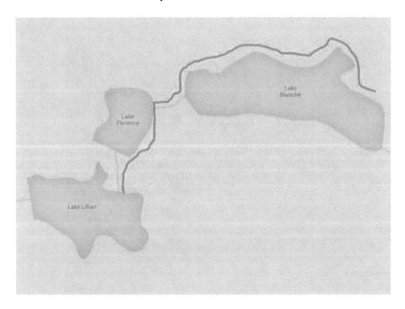

Lake Lillian Trail Map

FISHING INFORMATION:

The best time to fish these lakes is at ice off and in the fall. In the spring the lakes have just emerged from 7 months of ice and darkness and the fish are ravenous and eager to bite. Concentrate your fishing efforts on areas around the inlet stream and close to the bank. The fish will stack up near the inlet stream in the spring to snatch up food and nutrients being washed into the lake from the spring runoff. The influx of new water also replenishes the dwindled oxygen supply in the lake.

On a recent spring trip to the area my buddy and I caught 53 fat brook trout in a couple of hours. When we crested the knoll overlooking Lake Blanche, the surface of the water was boiling with the ripples of rising trout. We caught these fish on an assortment of jigs, lures and flies. It would have been possible at the peak of this feeding frenzy to use bare hooks with similar success. This is what makes spring fishing so wonderful at Lake Blanche.

One of the most successful methods to entice ice off Brookies is to fish with a 1/16 ounce mini-tube jigs. Your best luck will be with jigs in the following colors: white, red with white legs and a yellow.

Summer fishing can be more difficult than spring or fall. In the summer when the water warms up the fish head back down to the cooler water in the deepest sections of the lake. When fishing this lake during the heat of the summer it is important to adjust your fishing methods. If possible, fish early in the morning or late in the afternoon and evening. Fly fishing during the summer can be rewarding. During the summer, hatches of May flies and midges occur and terrestrials such as grasshoppers, beetles and ants end up in the lake and on the trout's menu. Attractor patterns such as Royal Wulffs and Renegades will produce fish when no hatch is present.

If fly fishing isn't your cup of tea then lures can be just as effective. One of the benefits of fishing with lures is that you can cast farther from the bank and into deeper water. Lures are also effective when

81

fished from a float tube. In the summer use a #1 or #2 Lil-Jake, Crocodile, or Mepps spinner and fish them deep. It has been our experience that the Brook Trout in this lake will follow lures to the shore before they strike. When this happens your mind will begin to race, your body will begin to jerk wildly, and you will be unable to control your arm causing premature lure ejection. If you find yourself in this situation take a deep breath and continue to retrieve the lure at the same pace, many fish will strike the lure before it gets to the shore out of fear of losing their meal.

The fall is another excellent time to fish these lakes. The hike through the canyon with its walls brilliantly splashed in fall colors will excite your senses as will the fiery colors of the spawning brook trout. The fish that inhabit high mountain lakes instinctively know that their watery world will soon be capped with several feet of ice and snow. In order to survive the winter they need to gorge themselves with as much food as their stomachs can hold and then some. This provides the angler the opportunity to catch nice size Brook Trout on a consistent basis. Brook Trout, like Brown Trout spawn in the fall. When fishing these lakes in the fall concentrate on the area around the inlet streams, fish will gather near this area in anticipation of the spawn. Fly fishing to these fish can be deadly with a small egg pattern or egg sucking leach. In the fall, the fish will also frequent the near shore areas in search of food. Jigs and lures should be fished similar to spring. If you are fishing with a dry fly, concentrate on those fish that are rising. Fall fishing can be both beautiful and productive and is definitely worth the hike.

The lakes in this basin are stocked on a consistent basis and the fish are very prolific. In fact, Brook Trout are so successful at reproducing that these lakes will become overpopulated with fish unless some are harvested. Over population would result in a limited food supply and stunted fish so take a few for the skillet.

The following map is of Lake Blanche. The red pins indicate locations where we have had productive fishing in the past. The next two maps are of Lake Florence and Lake Lillian. The red pins once again represent productive fishing locations.

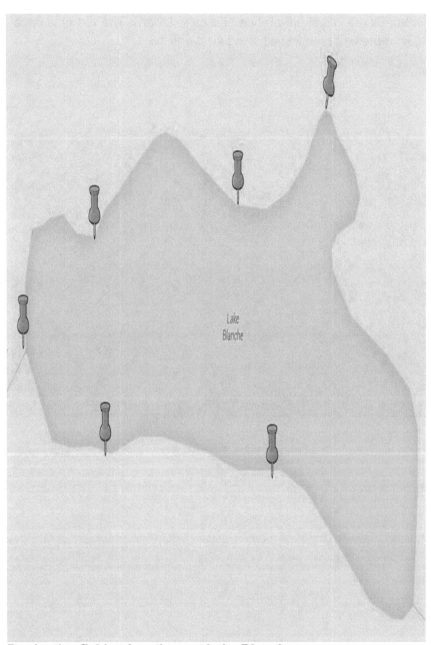

Productive fishing locations at Lake Blanche.

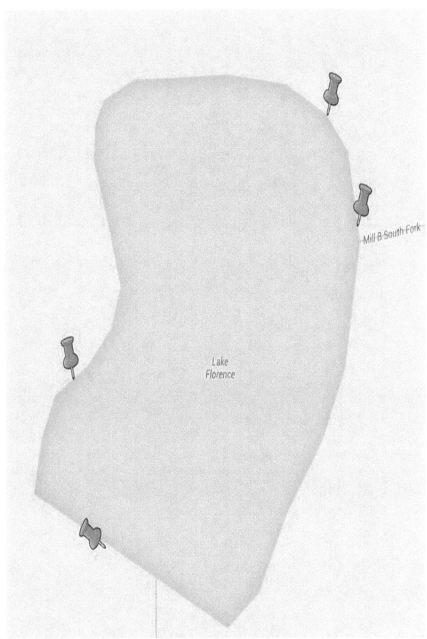

Mill B South Fork

Lake
Florence

Productive fishing locations at Lake Florence

85

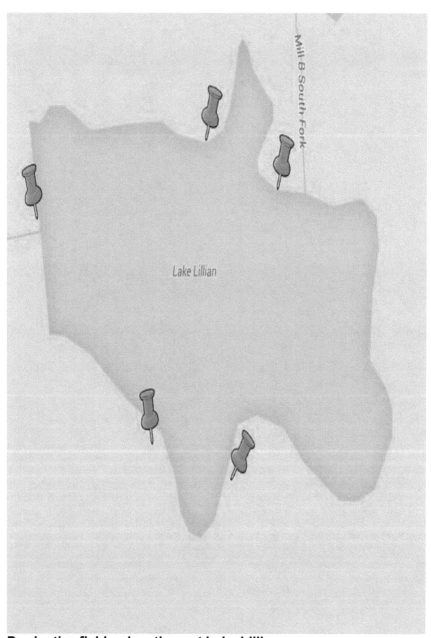

Productive fishing locations at Lake Lillian

CAMPING:

These lakes are close enough to Salt Lake and the hike short enough not to require an overnight stay. If you wish to camp near these lakes remember that you are in a watershed and a wilderness area. You must camp at least 200 feet from the water and no open fires are allowed in a wilderness area. The best place to camp is on the North side of Lake Blanche. This area is mostly smooth rock with several flat areas that have been used for camping in the past. It also provides an excellent view of the Salt Lake valley. If you want to cook a fresh trout for dinner it will be necessary to pack in a small cook stove.

These lakes play an important role in the supply of water to nearly a million people. Swimming, washing, and cleaning dishes in the water is prohibited. Don't put anything in the water you don't want coming out of your tap. Speaking of water, bring plenty of it, especially in the summer. If you need to drink water out of these lakes or streams make sure you boil it, filter it or chemically treat it to kill all girardia present.

TIP FOR THE LAKE BLANCHE BASIN:

Over the years I have learned to judge ice off on these lakes by watching Silver Lake in Brighton. When the ice comes off on Silver Lake it is a sure sign that Blanche should be ice free within a couple of days. If you want fast fishing for fat Brook trout make it a point to fish this lake early in the spring and again in the fall.

THE LAKE RATING

A.   AESTHETICS: The trail to Lake Blanche is one of the most beautiful areas in the Wasatch. The Lake itself is framed by Sun Dial Peak and is reminiscent of a lake in the Swiss Alps. However, this area receives extensive use and can be crowed on weekends. We recommend you fish this lake during the week to avoid the crowds and enhance your fishing experience.

B. ACCESSIBILITY: The hike to this lake is steep and can be hard for those anglers that are not in shape. If you're not in the best of shape we recommend that you take breaks and enjoy the scenery. If you are in relatively good shape this hike is still somewhat difficult with an elevation gain of 2700 feet. Bring plenty of water especially in the summer. A water purifier would work well and will reduce the amount of weight you carry.

C. OVERALL RATING: (Good)

LAKE MARY

Lake Florence (Photo Courtesy of Eric Bean)

ELEVATION: 8755 feet above sea level.

ICE OFF: Ice-off generally occurs during the last week of June or the first week of July.

HIKING MILES: Approximately 0.75 miles

HIKING TIME: ½ hour

AVERAGE SIZE OF FISH: Lake Mary is known for its hungry population of brook trout. The average fish will be 9 inches with some stretching the measuring tape over 12 inches. There are some very big Lake Trout in this lake. They are hard to catch but it is possible to do so.

WILDERNESS AREA: No wilderness designation, watershed area.

FISH SPECIES PRESENT: Brook trout and some Lake Trout in the deepest sections of the lake.

STOCKING SCHEDULE: This Lake is stocked by plane every other year. Check with the Utah Division of Wildlife Resources for the stocking schedule for this lake.

 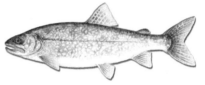

HOW TO GET THERE:

The trail to Lake Mary begins at the Brighton Ski Resort parking lot. Park in the resort parking area and proceed on the road between the Alpine Rose building and the Lodge. Follow this road until you come to the small stream. The Brighton Lakes trail head begins here. The trail follows the stream up the mountain for about ¾ of a mile. This section of trail is fairly steep but the trail is well maintained. The trail is situated in the fir trees. As you proceed up the mountain, on your left will be Brighton's Mary lift. This man made meadow attracts many of the local wildlife. If you are on the trail early in the morning or in the evening you may be lucky enough to see moose, deer and elk happily grazing. We have also seen Scat "droppings" from what appeared to be coyotes and black bears in this area. These are not the only "droppings" you might run into. Quite a few skiers leave behind valuables from the many "yard sales" they have on these slopes every ski season. Keep your eyes open, you never know what you might find. As you get near the end of the ski run you will notice a trail on your left. This trail heads up the hill to the top of the ridge. Once at the top, you will be at the Dog Lake Junction. Dog Lake is a short distance straight ahead. This lake is very shallow and contains no fish. At the Dog Lake junction you will turn right and follow the trail approximately a half-mile to the Lake Mary dam. The trail takes you along the base of the dam and then climbs up to the lake.

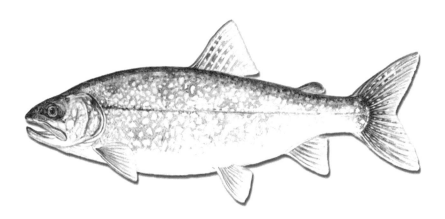

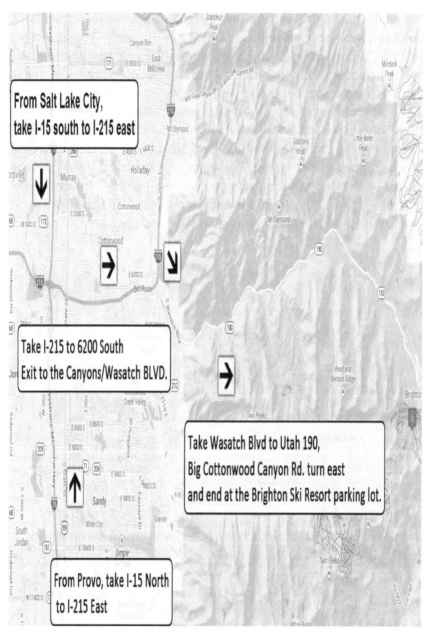

Driving directions to Lake Mary

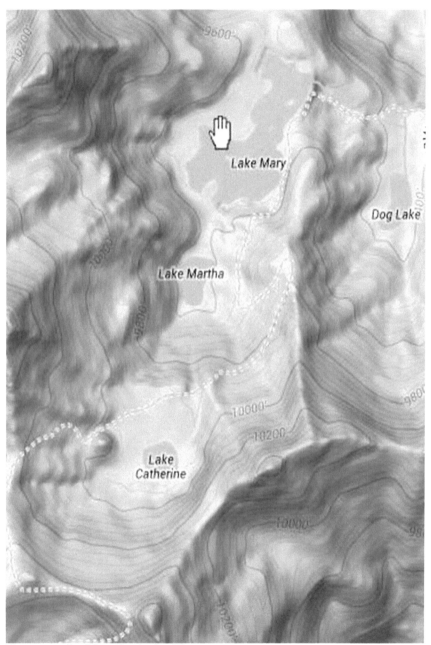

Topography Map for Lake Mary

93

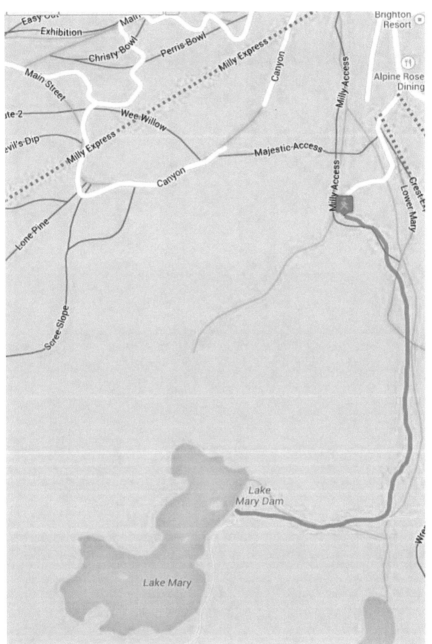

Trail Map for Lake Mary

FISHING LAKE MARY:

There are two things that stand out about the brook trout in Lake Mary, hungry and plentiful. This lake holds significant populations of brook trout that are not shy about taking your fly or lure. Lake Mary also has an elusive population of large lake trout in the deepest sections of this lake. While I have never caught one of these deep water monoliths in this lake, the Utah Division of Wildlife Resources has caught a few in their gill net surveys.

Lake Mary is a deep alpine reservoir which is used to regulate the water shed in this area. There are a lot of boulder, trees and willows around the edges of the lake.

Fly Fishers will find their best success casting to rising fish in the early morning and evening hours. During the spring and fall the fish will be close into shore and will cruise the shallow areas looking for any hatches or terrestrials that might be on the water. This is the best time for dry fly action. Nymphs and streamers work extremely well on this lake and produce fish when there is no surface activity. My favorite two nymph patterns are prince nymphs and damsel fly streamers.

Jig fishing is also very productive on this lake. When fishing in the spring and fall, concentrate on the East shore and near the Dam. Cast your jig into the deep water and retrieve through the submerged boulders and other structure. The brook trout will be near this structure waiting to pounce on their next meal.

Lures and spinners will work best during the heat of the summer. The extra weight that these lures provide will allow you to cast into the deep, black depths of this lake. As with most alpine lakes full of brook trout, the dog days of summer are not always the best time to be catching fish. If you are going to fish this lake during the summer, make sure you are there before the sun hits the water and don't leave until just before dark.

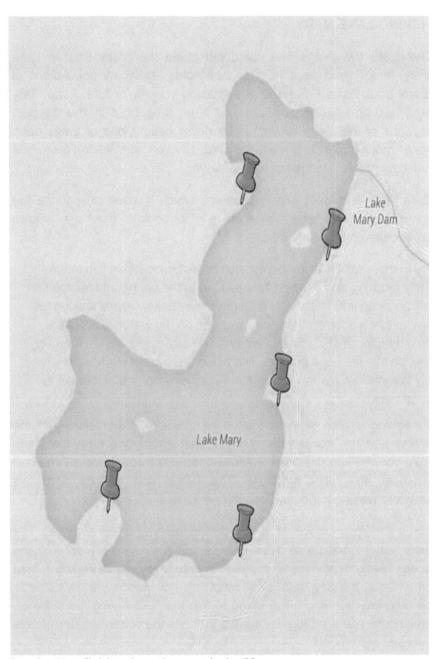

Productive fishing locations at Lake Mary

CAMPING:

There are a few campsites around this lake. Check with the forest service for campfire restrictions.

Take precautions during afternoon thunderstorms. You will be the tallest object around so get down and take cover until the storm passes. Whatever you do, don't be waving your fishing rod in the air trying to catch that last fish. If you do, that fish could very well be your last!

There is no spring water. Water is available from melting snow into July and may be obtained from the lake and stream. All water should be boiled or filtered before use.

TIP FOR LAKE MARY:

Make it a point to fish this lake early in the spring just after the ice has come off. With the ease of access and the number of hungry brook trout, this lake will provide you with some early, fast action on feisty trout.

THE LAKES RATING

A. AESTHETICS – The trail to Lake Mary is short and fairly easy. This trail is a beautiful hike with a lot of wildflowers in bloom during the months of June and July. Be prepared to see moose on your hike to this lake.

B. ACCESSIBILTY - Easy hike. The trail can be crowded with other hikers and fisherman on weekends.

C. OVERALL RATING. – A very beautiful hike especially during wildflower season. The fishing is outstanding for Brook Trout and there is that chance you might hook into a big lake trout..

LAKE MARTHA

ELEVATION: 8800 feet above sea level.

ICE OFF: Ice-off generally occurs during the last week of June or the first week of July.

HIKING MILES: Just under 1 mile

HIKING TIME: 45 minutes

AVERAGE SIZE OF FISH: The average fish you will catch in Lake Mary is 9 inches.

WILDERNESS AREA: No wilderness designation, watershed area.

FISH SPECIES PRESENT: Brook trout

STOCKING SCHEDULE: This Lake is stocked by plane every other year. Check with the Utah Division of Wildlife Resources for the stocking schedule for this lake.

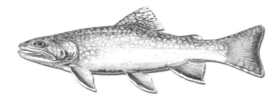

HOW TO GET THERE:

The trail to Lake Martha begins at the Brighton Ski Resort parking lot. Park in the resort parking area and proceed on the road between the Alpine Rose building and the Lodge. Follow this road until you come to the small stream. The Brighton Lakes trail head begins here. The trail follows the stream up the mountain for about ¾ of a mile. This section of trail is fairly steep but the trail is well maintained. The trail is situated in the fir trees. As you proceed up the mountain, on your left will be Brighton's Mary lift. This man made meadow attracts many of the local wildlife. If you are on the trail early in the morning or in the evening you may be lucky enough to see moose, deer and elk happily grazing. We have also seen Scat "droppings" from what appeared to be coyotes and black bears in this area. These are not the only "droppings" you might run into. Quite a few skiers leave behind valuables from the many "yard sales" they have on these slopes every ski season. Keep your eyes open, you never know what you might find. As you get near the end of the ski run you will notice a trail on your left. This trail heads up the hill to the top of the ridge. Once at the top, you will be at the Dog Lake Junction. Dog Lake is a short distance straight ahead. This lake is very shallow and contains no fish. At the Dog Lake junction you will turn right and follow the trail approximately a half-mile to the Lake Mary dam. The trail takes you along the base of the dam and then climbs up to the lake. From Lake Mary follow the trail a short distance to Lake Martha.

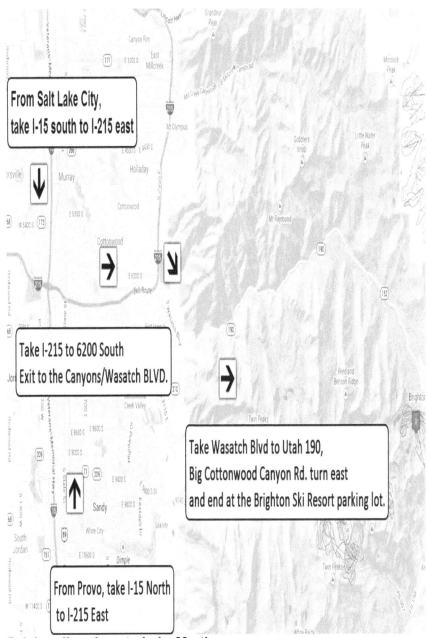

From Salt Lake City,
take I-15 south to I-215 east

Take I-215 to 6200 South
Exit to the Canyons/Wasatch BLVD.

Take Wasatch Blvd to Utah 190,
Big Cottonwood Canyon Rd. turn east
and end at the Brighton Ski Resort parking lot.

From Provo, take I-15 North
to I-215 East

Driving directions to Lake Martha

101

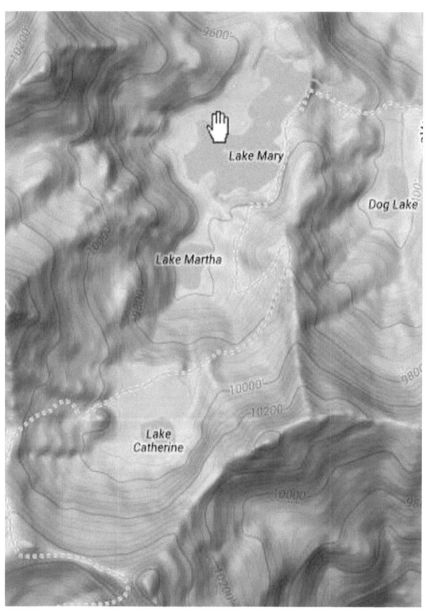

Topography Map for Lake Martha

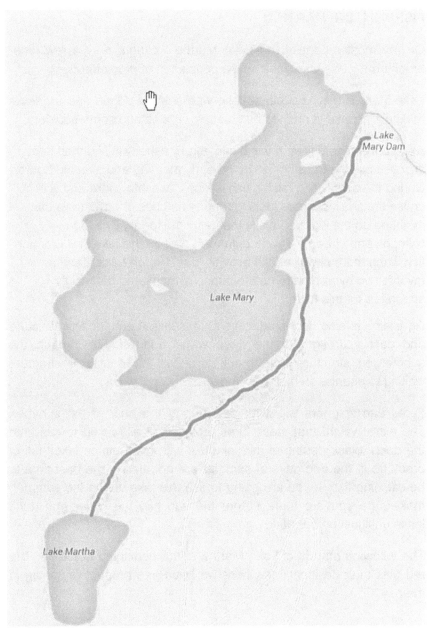

Trail Map to Lake Martha

103

FISHING LAKE MARTHA:

On my most recent trip to Lake Martha I caught only a few small brook trout. This lake does hold a population of brook trout.

Lake Mary is a typical alpine lake with shallow edges and a deeper middle. The lake is rimmed by grasses, willows and some boulders.

As with the other lakes in this basin, the fly fisher will find their best success casting to rising fish in the early morning and evening hours. During the spring and fall the fish will be close into shore and will cruise the shallow areas looking for any hatches or terrestrials that might be on the water. This is the best time for dry fly action. Nymphs and streamers work extremely well on this lake and produce fish when there is no surface activity. Just like on Lake Mary my favorite two nymph patterns are prince nymphs and damsel fly streamers for this lake...

Jig fishing is also very productive on this lake. Look for any structure and cast your jig into the deep water and retrieve through the submerged structure. The brook trout will be near this structure waiting to pounce on their next meal.

Lures and spinners will work best during the heat of the summer. The extra weight that these lures provide will allow you to cast into the deep, black depths of this lake. As with most alpine lakes full of brook trout, the dog days of summer are not always the best time to be catching fish. If you are going to fish this lake during the summer, make sure you are there before the sun hits the water and don't leave until just before dark.

The following map is of Lake Martha at the beginning of ice-off. The red pins indicate locations where we have had productive fishing in the past.

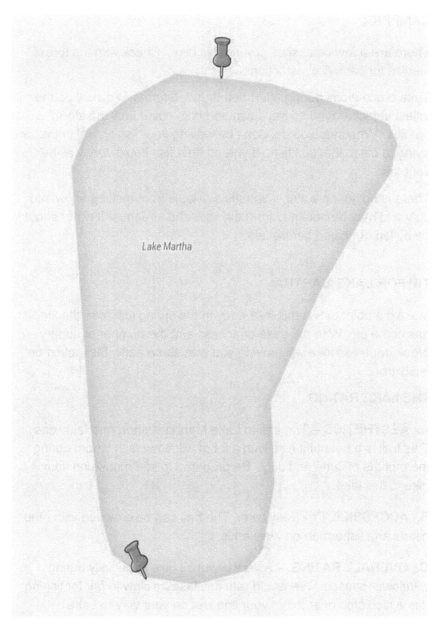

Productive fishing locations at Lake Martha

CAMPING:

There are a few campsites around this lake. Check with the forest service for campfire restrictions.

Take precautions during afternoon thunderstorms. You will be the tallest object around so get down and take cover until the storm passes. Whatever you do, don't be waving your fishing rod in the air trying to catch that last fish. If you do, that fish could very well be your last!

There is no spring water. Water is available from melting snow into July and may be obtained from the lake and stream. All water should be boiled or filtered before use.

TIP FOR LAKE MARTHA:

Make it a point to fish this lake early in the spring just after the ice has come off. With the ease of access and the number of hungry brook trout, this lake will provide you with some early, fast action on feisty trout.

THE LAKE RATING

A. AESTHETICS – The trail to Lake Martha is short and fairly easy. This trail is a beautiful hike with a lot of wildflowers in bloom during the months of June and July. Be prepared to see moose on your hike to this lake.

B. ACCESSIBILTY - Easy hike. The trail can be crowded with other hikers and fisherman on weekends.

C. OVERALL RATING. – A very beautiful hike especially during wildflower season. We would rate this lake as slow to fair for fishing. It is a nice stop over to get your line wet on your way to Lake Catherine.

LAKE CATHERINE

(Photo Courtesy of Mark Thomas)

ELEVATION: 9,950 feet above sea level.

ICE OFF: Ice-off generally occurs during the last week of June or the first week of July.

HIKING MILES: Approximately 2 miles.

HIKING TIME: 1 ½ hours.

AVERAGE SIZE OF FISH: Lake Catherine is known for its population of oversized brook trout. The average fish will be 11 inches with many stretching the measuring tape well past the 13-inch mark.

107

WILDERNESS AREA: No wilderness designation, watershed area.

FISH SPECIES PRESENT: Brook trout.

STOCKING SCHEDULE: This Lake is stocked by plane every other year. Check with the Utah Division of Wildlife Resources for the stocking schedule for this lake.

HOW TO GET THERE:

The trail to Lake Catherine begins at the Brighton Ski Resort parking lot. Park in the resort parking area and proceed on the road between the Alpine Rose building and the Lodge. Follow this road until you come to the small stream. The Brighton Lakes trail head begins here. The trail follows the stream up the mountain for about ¾ of a mile. This section of trail is fairly steep but the trail is well maintained. The trail is situated in the fir trees. As you proceed up the mountain, on your left will be Brighton's Mary lift. This man made meadow attracts many of the local wildlife. If you are on the trail early in the morning or in the evening you may be lucky enough to see moose, deer and elk happily grazing. We have also seen Scat "droppings" from what appeared to be coyotes and black bears in this area. These are not the only "droppings" you might run into. Quite a few skiers leave behind valuables from the many "yard sales" they have on these slopes every ski season. Keep your eyes open, you never know what you might find. As you get near the end of the ski run you will notice a trail on your left. This trail heads up the hill to the top of the ridge. Once at the top, you will be at the Dog Lake Junction. Dog Lake is a short distance straight ahead. This lake is very shallow and contains no fish. At the Dog Lake junction you will turn right and follow the trail approximately a half-mile to the Lake Mary dam. The trail takes you along the base of the dam and then climbs up to the lake. From Lake Mary, the trail will proceed along the east side of the lake and then turn to the south in the direction of Lake Martha. Lake Martha will be on your Left. Just past Lake Martha, the trail will turn to the left and ascend the ridge. From the top of the ridge you will be able to see Dog Lake on the east side and Lake Mary and Martha on the west. Continue following the ridge through the trees until you come to the junction of the Lake Catherine and Catherine Pass trails. The Catherine Pass trail continues straight while the trail to Lake Catherine turns to the left. It is a short hike to the lake from here.

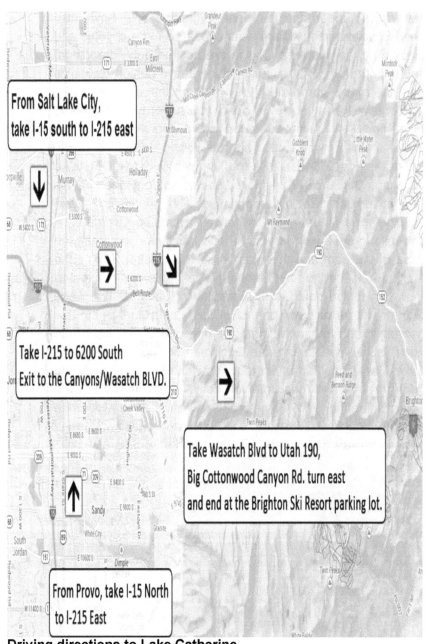

Driving directions to Lake Catherine

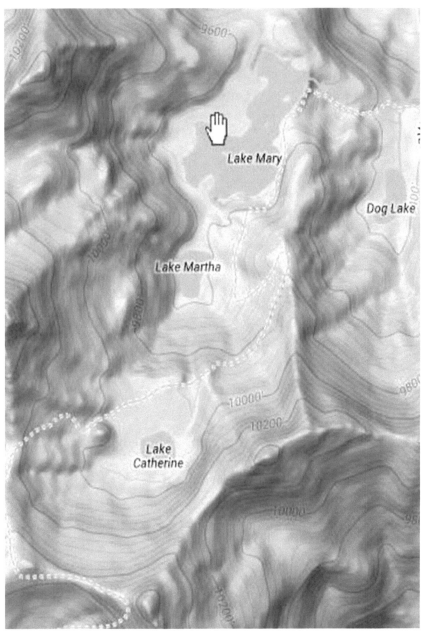

Lake Mary

Dog Lake

Lake Martha

Lake
Catherine

Topography Map for Lake Catherine

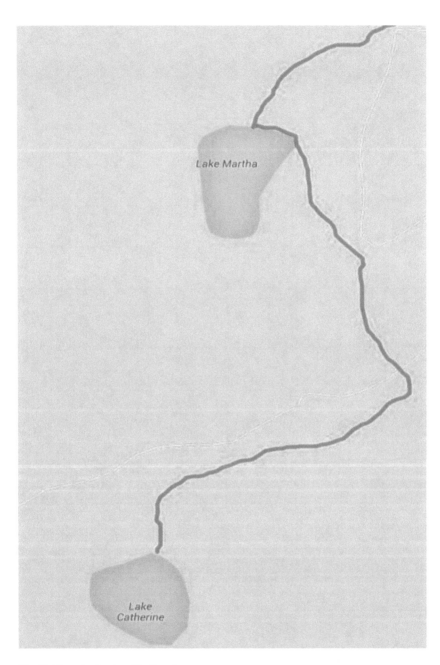

Trail Map to Lake Catherine

FISHING LAKE CATHERINE:

There is only one word to describe the brook trout in Lake Catherine, LARGE! This lake holds significant populations of hefty trout that are not shy about taking your fly or lure. Lake Catherine is a favorite of Fly Fishermen who enjoy catching 11 to 15-inch brook trout on dry flies.

Lake Catherine is a typical alpine lake, located in a cirque with a few pine trees around the edges and willows rimming many sections of the lake. The lake is shallow around the edges with a wide area of shallow water between the island and stream entrance on the southwest corner of the lake. The center of the lake is much deeper, providing cool water in the summer and protection from the ice in the winter. During severe winters, like the winters of 92-93, 96-97, and 2010-11 the lake will stay frozen for a longer period of time. During such severe winters, limited winter kill does have an effect on this lake. Many of the fish that die during these severe conditions are those which were unfortunate enough to be caught in the shallow sections of the lake when the water froze. Fortunately, this limited winter kill seems to have a positive effect on the remaining fish. When the population of fish is reduced it allows the remaining fish to take advantage of the increased food supply, oxygen and room in the lake. This would explain why the brook trout are larger in this lake than in many of the other lakes in the Wasatch.

Fly Fishers will find their best success casting to rising fish in the early morning and evening hours. During the spring and fall, the fish will be close into shore and will cruise the shallow areas looking for any hatches or terrestrials that might be on the water. This is the best time for dry fly action. Nymphs and streamers work extremely well on this lake and produce fish when there is no surface activity. Our favorite two nymph patterns are prince nymphs and damsel fly streamers.

Jig fishing is also very productive on this lake. When fishing in the spring and fall, concentrate on the northwest shore and near the

113

outlet stream of the lake. There is some deeper water in these two areas as well as underwater structure that the fish like. Cast your jig into the deep water and retrieve through the submerged boulders. The brook trout will be near this structure waiting to pounce on their next meal.

Lures and spinners will work best during the heat of the summer. The extra weight that these lures provide will allow you to cast into the deep, black depths of this lake. As with most alpine lakes full of brook trout, the dog days of summer are not always the best time to be catching fish. If you are going to fish this lake during the summer, make sure you are there before the sun hits the water and don't leave until just before dark. During the afternoon, we recommend you enjoy the warm summer day, the peace and quiet of the alpine setting and maybe even take a nap!

The following map is of Lake Catherine. The red pins indicate locations where I have had productive fishing in the past when the lake is ice free. This could be as late as July 4th depending on the severity of the previous winter and spring.

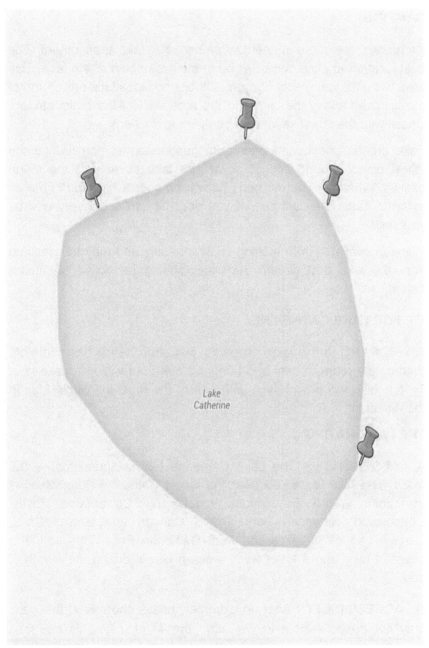

Productive fishing locations at Lake Catherine

CAMPING:

Campsites are more numerous around this lake than others. The best location to pitch camp will be in the area south of the lake. This area will offer you plenty of room. Other good locations are on top of the hill overlooking the lake and the area east of the outlet stream. Check with the forest service for campfire restrictions.

Take precautions during afternoon thunderstorms. You will be the tallest object around so get down and take cover until the storm passes. Whatever you do, don't be waving your fishing rod in the air trying to catch that last fish. If you do, that fish could very well be your last!

Water is available from melting snow into July and may be obtained from the lake and stream. All water should be boiled or filtered before use.

TIP FOR LAKE CATHERINE:

Take a fly rod to this lake, especially just after the ice has come off. With ample room to cast and hungry brook trout willing to take your fly, this lake will provide you with one of the most enjoyable trips in the Wasatch.

THE LAKE RATING

A. AESTHETICS - The Lake Catherine trail is approximately 2.6 miles. The lake is located near the top of Catherine Pass which is the point where 5 canyons meet. Big Cottonwood, Little Cottonwood, American Fork, Provo Canyon and Snake Creek Canyon can all be accessed from Catherine Pass. This trail is a beautiful hike with a lot of wildflowers in bloom during the month of July.

B. ACCESSIBILTY - After an extremely heavy snow year, this pass may not be accessible to well after the 4th of July. This trail is a segment of the Great Western Trail. This area is also popular with

116

Moose. Do not approach moose if you encounter them on the. Also, never get between a mother moose and her babies! Give these animals plenty of space and enjoy them from a safe distance. The hike to the lake is strenuous for those people that might be out of shape.

C. **OVERALL RATING.** – A very beautiful hike especially during wildflower season. The fishing is outstanding for large brook trout. This lake offers fly fishers the best experience of all the high lakes in the Wasatch.

DOG LAKE *"BRIGHTON"*

Dog Lake (Photo Courtesy of Eric Bean)

ELEVATION: 8,810 feet above sea level.

ICE OFF: Ice-off generally occurs during the last week of June or the first week of July.

WILDERNESS AREA: No wilderness designation, watershed area.

HIKING MILES: Approximately 1 mile.

HIKING TIME: 45 minutes.

WILDERNESS AREA:

FISH SPECIES PRESENT: Lake is full of Tiger Salamanders and is

118

not deep enough or suitable for fish.

HOW TO GET THERE

The trail head is located in between the Brighton Ski Lodge and The Crest Express. At the trail head itself the trail will split two ways. Take the one to the LEFT. The trail will start by gaining some uphill while gradually veering in the direction of the lake. After passing a log that has been converted into a bench, a very well marked trail junction will appear. From here it is your choice on which lake you wish to visit. Dog Lake is a quick left from this junction

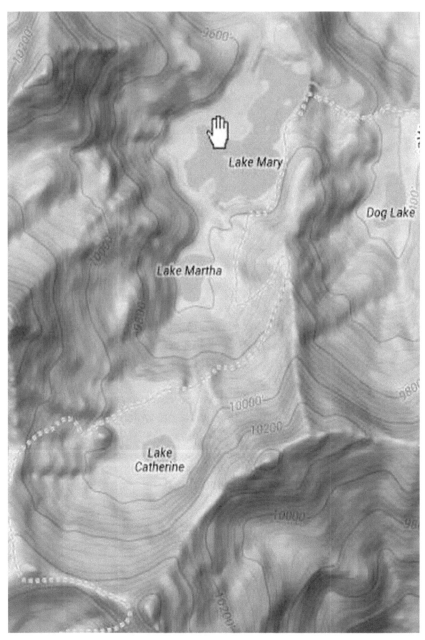

Topography Map of Dog Lake "Brighton"

120

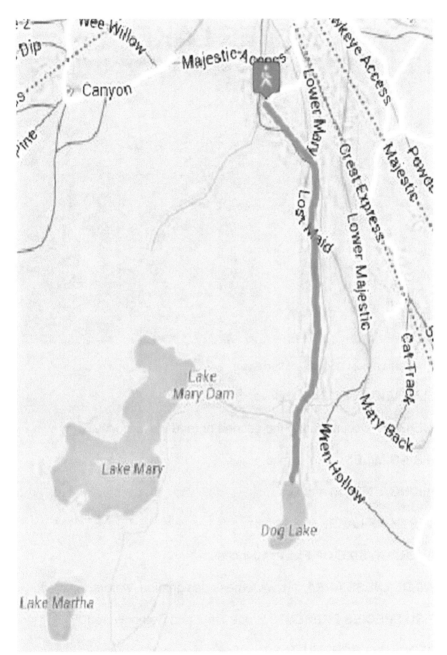

Trail Map to Dog Lake "Brighton"

121

SILVER LAKE

Silver Lake (Photo Courtesy of Eric Bean)

ELEVATION: 8712 feet above sea level.

ICE OFF: Occurs during the second or third week in May.

HIKING MILES: ¼ of a mile.

HIKING TIME: 10 minutes.

DEPTH OF LAKE: 11 – 14 feet

AVERAGE SIZE OF FISH: 10 inches

WILDERNESS AREA: No wilderness designation, watershed area.

FISH SPECIES PRESENT: Brook Trout and Rainbow trout.

STOCKING SCHEDULE: This Lake is a very popular lake and is easy to access for fishermen. It gets heavy fishing pressure during

122

the week and on weekends. It is also a very popular location for hikers, picnics and photography. The lake is stocked several times during the spring, summer and fall fishing season. Check the Utah Division of Wildlife Resources for specific stocking dates. The lake is stocked by truck.

HOW TO GET THERE:

Silver Lakes' parking lot is located approximately 15 miles up big cottonwood canyon. Follow the canyon road until you reach the Brighton Loop. The parking lot is located near the beginning of this loop, directly west of the Brighton General Store. The trail to the lake begins at the Solitude Nordic Visitors Center. From the Visitors center it is a short walk to the lake.

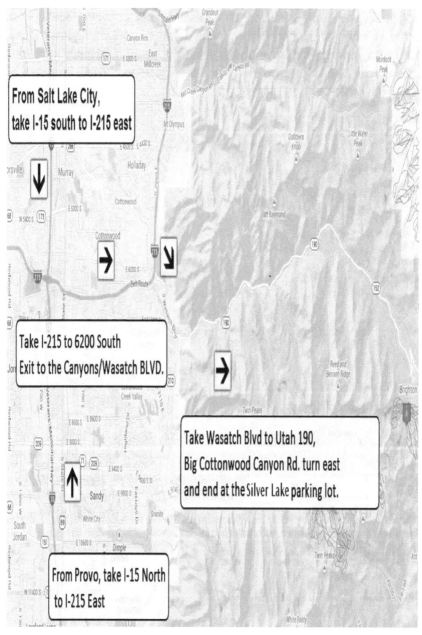

From Salt Lake City, take I-15 south to I-215 east

Take I-215 to 6200 South Exit to the Canyons/Wasatch BLVD.

Take Wasatch Blvd to Utah 190, Big Cottonwood Canyon Rd. turn east and end at the Silver Lake parking lot.

From Provo, take I-15 North to I-215 East

Driving directions to Silver Lake "Brighton"

124

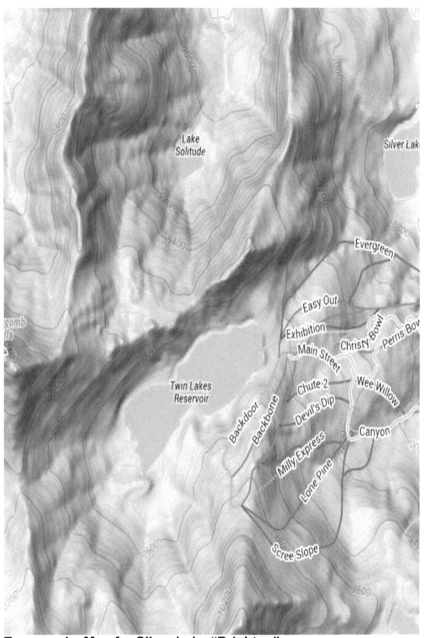

Topography Map for Silver Lake "Brighton"

125

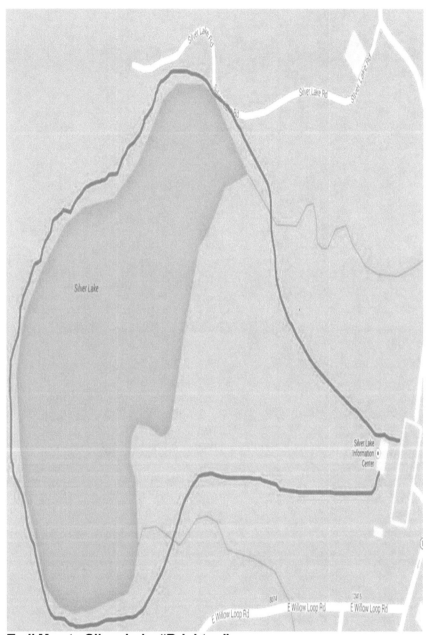

Trail Map to Silver Lake "Brighton"

126

FISHING SILVER LAKE:

Silver Lake is the most accessible and popular fishing destination in the Wasatch. There are many factors that attributed to the popularity of this lake such as frequent stocking by the Department of Wildlife Resources, easy access from Salt Lake City, and beautiful scenery. This lake also provides anglers with an excellent opportunity to include their families and teach the kids how to fish. If you are the type of person who prefers to fish in areas that are secluded and quiet you should either avoid this lake or lighten up and enjoy the company of your fellow fishing community.

The trail head, which begins at the Nordic Center, is well maintained and provides fisherman with easy and level walking. Walking and wading staffs are not necessary on this water. Several years ago the forest service installed a system of wood boardwalks to protect this fragile alpine meadow from ever increasing foot traffic and use. These boardwalks elevate the hiker above this alpine meadow and interpretive signs placed along the boardwalk offer information on the flora and fauna found in the lake and meadow. There are several platforms which extend into the lake and provide access to areas which otherwise would be inaccessible. These platforms have proved popular, especially on weekends when fishermen stand elbow to elbow in pursuit of their limit.

Silver lake is one of the first lakes to lose its ice cap in spring. When the ice finally recedes, fishing can be outstanding for small brook trout and hold over rainbows. As with many of the lakes covered in this book, spring is a good time to use jigs and flies. The patterns cover in this book work well on this lake. However, one particular pattern seems to work especially well on this lake during spring. Damsel flies fished from a float tube are an excellent spring combination.

Fly Fishers will find their best success casting to rising fish in the early morning and evening hours. During the spring and fall the fish will be close into shore and will cruise the shallow areas looking for any hatches or terrestrials that might be on the water. This is the best time for dry fly action. Nymphs and streamers work extremely well on this lake and produce fish when there is no surface activity. Our favorite two nymph patterns are prince nymphs and damsel fly streamers.

Jig fishing is also very productive on this lake. When fishing in the spring and fall, concentrate on the northwest shore and near the outlet stream of the lake. There is some deeper water in these two areas as well as underwater structure that the fish like. Cast your jig into the deep water and retrieve through the submerged boulders. The brook trout will be near this structure waiting to pounce on their next meal.

Lures and spinners will work best during the heat of the summer. The extra weight that these lures provide will allow you to cast into the deep, black depths of this lake. As with most alpine lakes full of brook trout, the dog days of summer are not always the best time to be catching fish. If you are going to fish this lake during the summer, make sure you are there before the sun hits the water and don't leave until just before dark.

The following map is of Silver Lake. The red pins indicate locations where we have had productive fishing in the past.

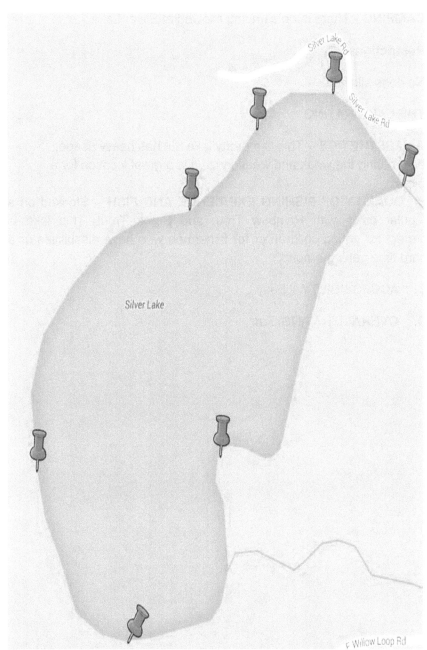

Productive fishing locations at Silver Lake "Brighton"

CAMPING - There is no camping allowed at Silver Lake.

Restrictions

No dogs allowed.

THE LAKE RATING

A. AESTHETICS – This is a pretty lake but has heavy usage, both during the week and weekends. It is a great location for a picnic.

B. OUALITY OF FISHING EXPRIENCE AND FISH – Stocked on a regular basis with Rainbow Trout and Brook Trout. This lake is perfect for young children or for fishermen who have disabilities or a hard time getting around.

C. ACCESSIBILTY – Easy

D. OVERALL RATING. Fair

TWIN LAKES

Twin Lakes (Photo Courtesy of Eric Bean)

ELEVATION: **9480** feet above sea level.

ICE OFF: Occurs during the second or third week in May.

HIKING MILES: 2.5 miles round trip

HIKING TIME: Approximately one hour.

AVERAGE SIZE OF FISH: 10 - 12 inches

WILDERNESS AREA: No wilderness designation, watershed area.

FISH SPECIES PRESENT: Cutthroat Trout

STOCKING SCHEDULE: This reservoir does receive some

131

pressure as it is easy for fishermen access. It is also a very popular location for hikers, picnics and photography. The lake is stocked with cutthroat trout. Check the Utah Division of Wildlife Resources for specific stocking dates. The lake is stocked by truck.

HOW TO GET THERE:

Twin Lakes/Silver Lakes' parking lot is located approximately 15 miles up big cottonwood canyon. Follow the canyon road until you reach the Brighton Loop. The parking lot is located near the beginning of this loop, directly west of the Brighton General Store. The trail to the lake begins at the Solitude Nordic Visitors Center. From the Visitors center it is a short walk to silver lake. The hike to Twin Lakes is 2.5 miles round trip from the parking area, along an easy, well-marked trail.

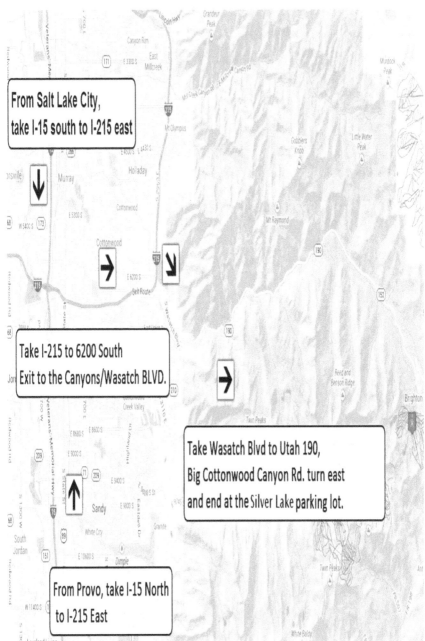

From Salt Lake City, take I-15 south to I-215 east

Take I-215 to 6200 South Exit to the Canyons/Wasatch BLVD.

Take Wasatch Blvd to Utah 190, Big Cottonwood Canyon Rd. turn east and end at the Silver Lake parking lot.

From Provo, take I-15 North to I-215 East

Driving Directions to Twin Lakes

133

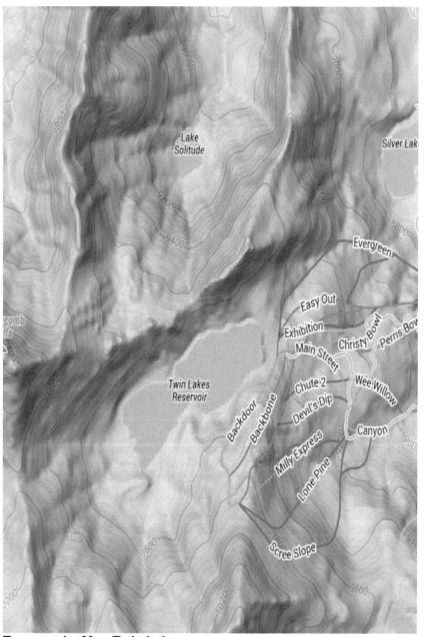

Topography Map Twin Lakes

134

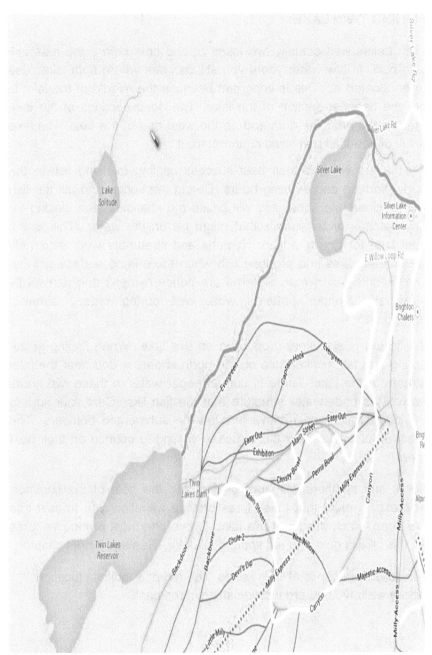

Trail Map to Twin Lakes

135

FISHING TWIN LAKE:

Twin Lakes was actually two lakes at one time before the reservoir was built. In low water years you still can see where both lakes use to be located at. This is important because the middle of the lake is not the deepest section of the lake. The deep sections of the lake are located near the dam and on the west end of the lake. The lake is full of beautiful pan sized cutthroat trout.

Fly Fishers will find their best success casting to rising fish in the early morning and evening hours. During the spring and fall the fish will be close into shore and will cruise the shallow areas looking for any hatches or terrestrials that might be on the water. This is the best time for dry fly action. Nymphs and streamers work extremely well on this lake and produce fish when there is no surface activity. Our favorite two nymph patterns are prince nymphs and damsel fly streamers. Hopper patterns work well during breezy summer afternoons.

Jig fishing is also very productive on this lake. When fishing in the spring and fall, concentrate on the north shoreline and near the inlet stream of the lake. There is some deeper water in these two areas as well as underwater structure that the fish like. Cast your jig into the deep water and retrieve through the submerged boulders. The brook trout will be near this structure waiting to pounce on their next meal.

Lures and spinners will work best during the heat of the summer. The extra weight that these lures provide will allow you to cast into the deep, black depths of this lake. One of the most productive lures on this lake is gold and red spotted Lil-Jake. See equipment chapter.

The following map is of Twin Lakes. The red pins indicate locations where we have had productive fishing in the past.

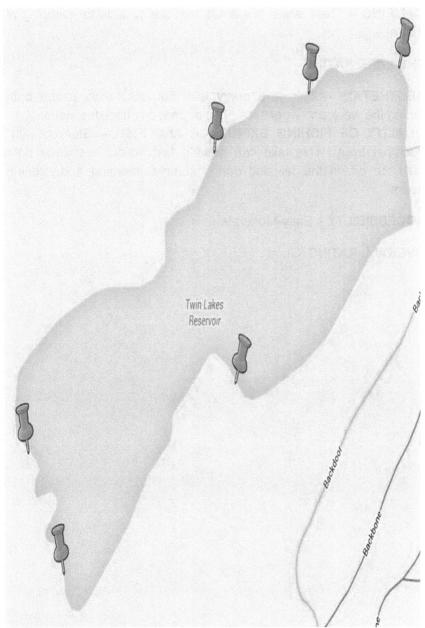

Productive fishing locations at Twin Lakes

CAMPING – There are a few areas that are suitable for camping at this lake.

THE LAKE RATING

AESTHETICS – This is a pretty lake but has heavy usage both during the week and weekends. It is a great day hike destination.

OUALITY OF FISHING EXPRIENCE AND FISH – Stocked with cutthroat trout... This lake can provide fast action, especially right after ice off, in the fall and during summer morning and evening hours.

ACCESSIBILTY – Easy-Moderate

OVERALL RATING. Good

DOG LAKE *"Mill Creek Drainage"*

Dog Lake (Photo Courtesy of Eric Bean.com)

ELEVATION: 8,810 feet above sea level.

ICE OFF: Ice-off generally occurs during the last week of June or the first week of July.

HIKING MILES: Approximately 2.5 mile round trip.

HIKING TIME: 1 ½ hours.

WILDERNESS AREA: Mount Olympus Wilderness Area.

FISH SPECIES PRESENT: Dog Lake is full of Tiger Salamanders and is not deep enough or suitable for fish.

This lake can be accesses from both Mill Creek and Big Cottonwood Canyon.

HOW TO GET THERE

The trail head is about 9 miles up Big Cottonwood Canyon and is just before the Spruces Campground, there is a large parking area on both sides of the road. The Dog Lake Trail begins next to the information booth in the center of the north side parking lot. Just follow the well maintained trail as it begins to climb northeast up the side of the mountain. After 1 3/4 miles you will notice some pipes in the stream that identify a spring. 150 yards after you pass the spring you will encounter a signed junction. The trail to the east (right) goes to Desolation Lake. Follow the trail to the west (left) towards Dog Lake. From the junction the trail climbs 1/2 mile to Dog Lake

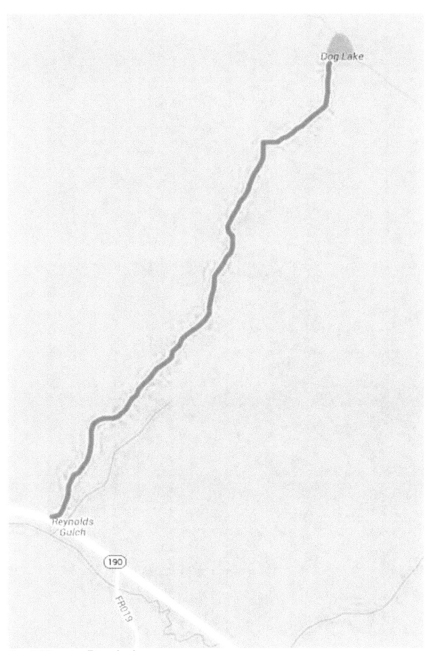

Trail Map to Dog Lake

Topography Map of Dog Lake

142

LAKE DESOLATION

Photo courtesy of Melinda Wickham

ELEVATION: 8,810 feet above sea level.

ICE OFF: Ice-off generally occurs during the last week of June or the first week of July.

HIKING MILES: Approximately 1 mile.

HIKING TIME: 45 minutes.

WILDERNESS AREA: No wilderness designation, watershed area.

FISH SPECIES PRESENT: Lake is full of Tiger Salamanders and is not deep enough or suitable for fish.

HOW TO GET THERE

The hike to Desolation Lake is moderate to hard. You should be in good shape for this hike or it could take you several hours to

complete. It is a popular one for both hikers and mountain bikers, and is busy on weekends.

The trail head is about 9 miles up Big Cottonwood Canyon and is just before the Spruces Campground, there is a large parking area on both sides of the road. The Mill D North Fork trail head is on the North side of the road.

From Mill D North Fork the trail climbs steadily through the trees. The trail is well marked and easy to follow. About 1.2 miles from the trail head is an area to sit by the creek. From this location it is about .7 miles to the fork for Dog Lake. Keep right as the sign indicates to continue to Desolation Lake. The last 1.8 miles to Desolation Lake levels out, though a few uphill climbs are still in front of you. At the end of the trail it will quickly decline down to the lake.

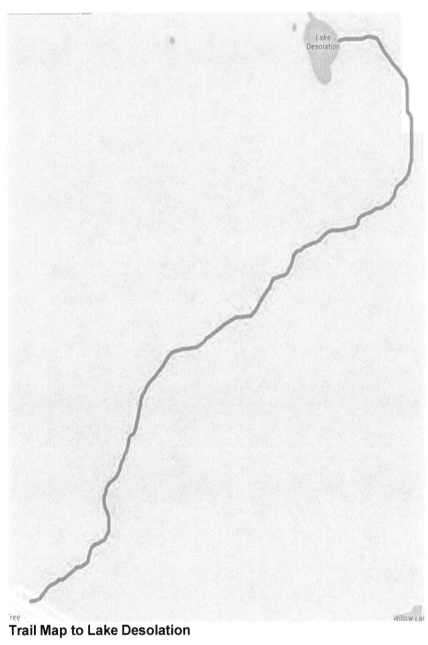

Trail Map to Lake Desolation

Topography Map of Lake Desolation

146

CHAPTER 7

THE LAKES OF

LITTLE COTTONWOOD

DRAINAGE

WHITE PINE LAKE, RED PINE LAKE, UPPER RED PINE LAKE,
LOWER BELLS CANYON RESERVOIR, UPPER BELLS CANYON
RESERVOIR CECRET LAKE

RED PINE LAKE AND UPPER RED PINE LAKE

RED PINE LAKE

Red Pine Lake (Photo Courtesy of Eric Bean)

ELEVATION: Lower Red Pine Lake - 9600 feet above sea level

UPPER RED PINE LAKE

Upper Red Pine Lake (Photo Courtesy of Eric Bean)

ELEVATION: Upper Red Pine Lake 10,000 feet above sea level.

ICE OFF: Upper and Lower Red Pine lakes are high alpine lakes where snow and ice last well into summer. Ice off will generally occur during the first week of July.

HIKING MILES: Lower Red Pine Lake – 3 miles. Upper Red Pine Lake – 3 ½ miles.

HIKING TIME: Lower Red Pine Lake – 2h 45m. Upper Red Pine Lake – 3 hours.

AVERAGE SIZE OF FISH: Upper Red Pine Lake contains very large Cutthroat trout with many fish over 5 pounds. Most fish we have

149

caught in this lake are over 13 inches with the majority in the 15 inch size range. Lower Red Pine Lake contains smaller cutthroats and some brook trout. This lake is drawn down considerably during the summer months and can be subject to winter kill if the water level is to low going into winter.

WILDERNESS AREA: Lone Peak Wilderness Area.

FISHING USAGE: On weekdays very few anglers are willing to hike to upper Red Pine Lake and fishing pressure is light during the week and on weekends. Lower Red Pine is a popular destination for hikers.

FISH SPECIES PRESENT: Cutthroat Trout and Brook Trout.

STOCKING SCHEDULE: Upper and Lower Red Pine Lake are stocked by plane every other year. Check with the Utah Division of Wildlife Resources for the stocking schedule for this lake.

HOW TO GET THERE:

Upper and Lower Red Pine Lakes are within the boundaries of the Wasatch National Forest and the Lone Peak wilderness. The trail is located 5.5 miles up Little Cottonwood Canyon at the White Pine

Trail head. The White Pine Trail head offers ample parking during the week but can be crowed on weekends. Forest Service restrooms and garbage receptacles are located at the parking area. To begin, follow the paved path down to Little Cottonwood Stream and cross the large wooden footbridge. Once you have crossed the stream proceed a short distance through a thick canopy of trees until you come to a wide dirt road. This road is used to maintain White Pine Dam. Follow this road approximately one mile until you come to White Pine Creek and the forest service directional sign. The trail to White Pine Lake branches off to the left. To continue to Lower Red Pine Lake it is necessary to walk upstream approximately 100 feet to the Forest Service footbridge and cross the stream. Once you have crossed the stream the trail is fairly flat and easy walking. This section of the trail takes you through a beautiful mixed forest of aspen, mountain mahogany, oak and pines. Approximately a ½ mile from the stream you will come to an overlook with spectacular views of the Salt Lake Valley. It is also possible from this vantage to see how the glaciers gave the canyon its distinctive U-shape. Once you pass the overlook you will be heading up Red Pine Canyon. Red Pine Creek will be some distance below the trail and difficult to see. From this point on, the easy stroll through the forest comes to an abrupt end. The trail steadily gets steeper and the difficulty increases. Once you have hiked a mile from the overlook you will reach Red Pine Creek and a pile of old mine tailings. Near the mine tailings a trail crosses the creek on a footbridge and leads to Maybird Gulch with its several small fish-less ponds. Do not cross the creek! The trail to Lower Red pine Lake is on the east side of the canyon and continues up through more pine and aspens for another ½ mile. This section of trail is beautiful in early summer when the wildflowers are in full bloom. As you reach the end of the trail you will crest the ridge and be able to see Lower Red Pine Lake in front of you. If your final destination is the monstrous cutthroats in Upper Red Pine Lake, follow the trail along the east side of the lake until you reach the north end near the inlet stream. On your left you will notice a path, which leads up the side of the mountain; this is the

151

trail to Upper Red Pine Lake. If you pass the small inlet stream you will have passed the turn-off. This section of trail is very steep and can be dangerous if you lose your footing. Follow this trail until you come to a boulder field. The trail will become less evident when you reach this boulder field so it will be necessary to pick your own way to the top. Extreme caution should be taken when crossing this boulder field in the rain. These rocks can get very slippery and a fall could ruin your whole day! Once you reach the top of this boulder field you will be able to see the lake. Upper Red Pine Lake is Located at the base of 11321 foot White Baldy Peak.

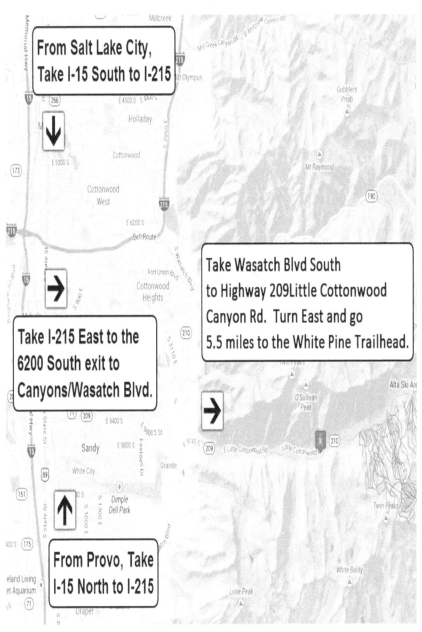

From Salt Lake City,
Take I-15 South to I-215

Take I-215 East to the
6200 South exit to
Canyons/Wasatch Blvd.

Take Wasatch Blvd South
to Highway 209Little Cottonwood
Canyon Rd. Turn East and go
5.5 miles to the White Pine Trailhead.

From Provo, Take
I-15 North to I-215

Driving directions to Red Pine and Upper Red Pine Lakes

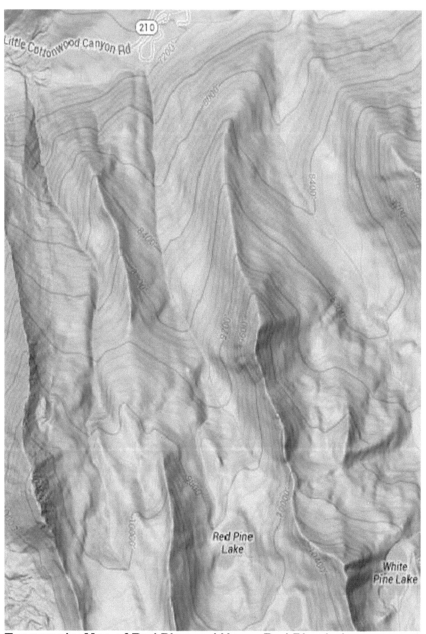

Topography Map of Red Pine and Upper Red Pine Lakes

154

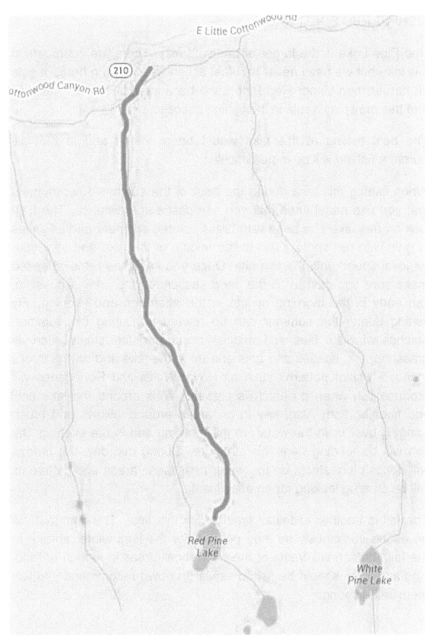

Trail Map to Red Pine and Upper Red Pine Lakes

155

FISHING RED PINE LAKE

Red Pine Lake is the larger of the two lakes. There are cutthroats in this lake but we have never had fast action when fishing here. It gets hit harder then Upper Red Pine Lake because it is easier to access and this may play a role in the fishing success.

The best fishing at this lake would be at ice-off and in the fall. Summer fishing will be more difficult.

When fishing this lake during the heat of the summer I recommend that you use metal lures that you can cast some distance. The best luck on this lake has been with brass colored spinners and Lil Jakes in gold with red spots. Cast to the middle of the lake and vary your retrieval speed until the fish bite. Once you know the retrieval speed make sure you cast to all the deep sections of the lake. If possible, fish early in the morning or late in the afternoon and evening. Fly fishing during the summer can be rewarding. During the summer, hatches of May flies and midges occur and terrestrials such as grasshoppers, beetles and ants end up in the lake and on the trout's menu. Attractor patterns such as Royal Wulffs and Renegades will produce fish when no hatch is present. Walk around the lake until you find the fish. Also, key in on areas around willows and brush hanging over or in the water. In the morning and in the evening, the fish will be feeding near this structure. During mid day, the breeze will deposit terrestrials on the water near these areas and cutthroats will be cruising looking for an easy meal.

The fall is another excellent time to fish this lake. The cutthroat will be eating voraciously as they prepare for the long winter ahead. In the fall, the fish will frequent the near shore areas in search of food. Jigs and lures should be fished similar to how I recommend you fish them in the spring.

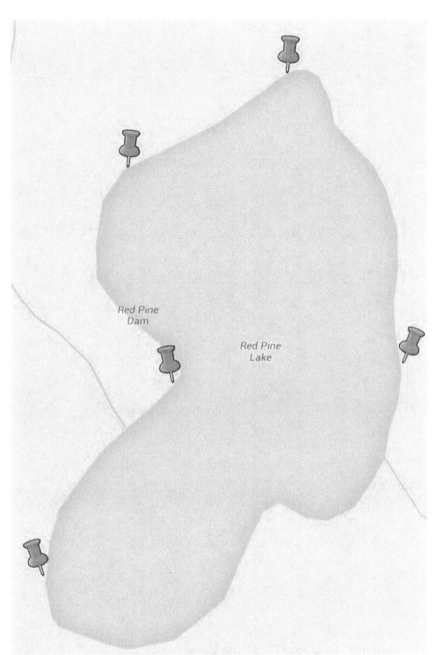

Productive fishing locations at Red Pine Lake

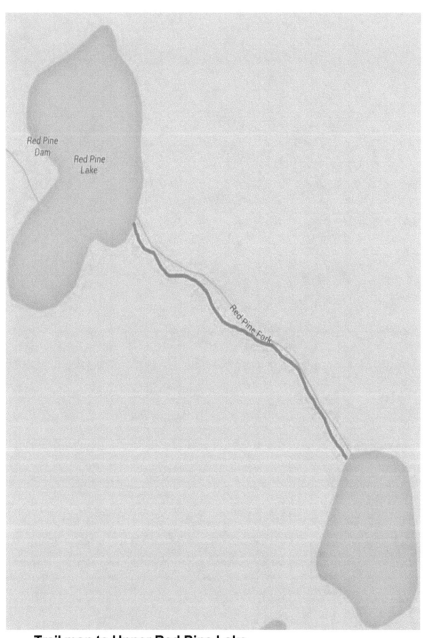

Trail map to Upper Red Pine Lake

FISHING UPPER RED PINE LAKE:

This is a very productive lake. The cutthroats in this lake grow big, fat and colorful. I have caught some fish in the 3-5-pound range and have seen bigger ones cruising the shoreline. It is rare to find a high mountain lake of this caliber so close to a major metropolitan area. It is because lakes like Upper Red Pine are so rare that I debated long and hard over whether or not I should let the secret of this lake be known. In the end I decided that since this is a book on fishing the Wasatch there was no choice but to include it. To those few fishermen who have guarded this lakes secret for many years, I apologize. To those who are just now learning about this lake please protect it by practicing catch and release on these monster cutthroats. If you want to eat a few, take the smaller ones home.

The best time to fish this lake is at Ice off, which is very late in the year. Cutthroats are most vulnerable in the spring when they swim out of the lakes and into small tributary streams to spawn. Upper Red Pine Lake does not have any tributary streams large enough to support a spawning run of cutthroats. This is bad for the Cutthroat but good for the fisherman. It is good for the fisherman because the trout are congregate near shore looking for a stream to spawn in making them easy targets for shore fishermen. In the spring, fishermen should concentrate near submerged boulders. There are many areas of this lake with submerged boulders. Our best success has been on the west shore near the boulder dam. Another good spot with lots of submerged boulders is on the north east side of the lake. But if you are after the 5+ pound fish the southeast corner of the lake is your best bet. This is a deep section of the lake with a sandy and boulder strewn shoreline. In early summer it is still hard to access this area of the lake because of deep snow, so be sure of you footing. The big trout are in deep drop offs near the shore.

I recommend that you use mini-jigs in red, white, black and gray colors during the spring and fall. During the short summer use metal lures such as Mepps, Crocodiles and Lil Jakes.

159

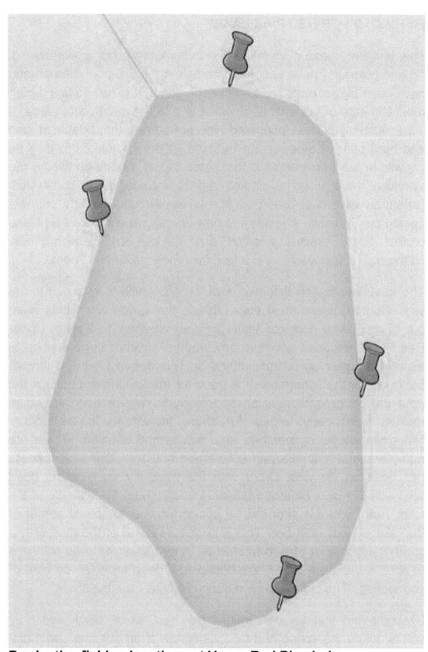

Productive fishing locations at Upper Red Pine Lake

CAMPING:

Camping sites are limited and are best situated on the southern and eastern sides of Red Pine Lake and at least 200 feet from the water. The Eastern side has several areas where people have camped and does provide excellent views of the lake. There is also evidence of ground fires in this area. Remember this is a wilderness area and ground fires are prohibited. If you camp on the Southern side of the lake it will be necessary to set up camp further from the lake because of the steep slope. It is not recommended to camp on the other areas around the lake because of the steep terrain and the inability to stay far enough away from the water.

If you camp at Upper Red Pine Lake there will be very little cover. Be careful during any thunderstorm in this area as you do not want to be struck by lightning.

Special precautions should be made at this lake to ensure a bear free camp. Black bears do inhabit the Wasatch and can be lured into your camp by the smell of a free meal.

Water is available from melting snow well in to July and water may be taken from the lake. All water from either snow melt or the lake should be either boiled or filtered.

TIP FOR UPPER RED PINE LAKE:

Early in the year, concentrate on the northern shoreline and the northwest corner of the lake. Make sure to fish near rocks and other underwater structure. Don't overlook areas you might think are too close to shore; I have caught fish within a foot of the shoreline. Try several jigs, lures and flies until you find the right pattern. As summer progresses the fish will retreat to the deeper water.

THE LAKE RATING

A. AESTHETICS – Beautiful hike to two very nice alpine lakes. You will forget how close you are to a major metropolitan city.

B. ACCESSIBILITY: Moderate to Lower Red Pine Lake. Difficult from Lower Red Pine to Upper Red Pine Lake.

C. OUALITY OF FISHING EXPRIENCE AND FISH – Lower Red Pine – Poor Upper Red Pine - Excellent for very large Cutthroat Trout.

C. OVERALL RATING. Good

WHITE PINE LAKE

White Pine Lake (Photo Courtesy of Eric Bean)

ELEVATION: 10,000 Feet above sea level.

ICE OFF: White Pine Lake is a high alpine lake where spring arrives late. Ice off will generally occur during the first week of July.

HIKING MILES: 4 ½ miles.

HIKING TIME: 3h 45m

AVERAGE SIZE OF FISH: White Pine Lake is home to large cutthroat trout. Most fish will be in the 12 to 15-inch range with some fish exceeding 18 inches.

WILDERNESS AREA: No wilderness designation, watershed area.

FISHING USAGE: If you want isolation, visit this lake during the week and you will probably be the only one on the lake. Weekends see light fishing pressure. This lake is a popular destination for hikers and bikers. White Pine Lake is not within a designated wilderness area so mountain biking is allowed.

FISH SPECIES PRESENT: Cutthroat Trout.

STOCKING SCHEDULE: This lake is stocked by plane every other year.

HOW TO GET THERE:

The hike to White Pine Lake is not extremely hard but it is long. It will take you close to four hours to reach this lake. If you are planning a day trip it is necessary to get an early start. The trail is located 5.5 miles up Little Cottonwood

164

Canyon at the White Pine Trail head. To begin, follow the paved path down to the stream and cross the large wooden footbridge. Once you have crossed the stream proceed a short distance to the graded road. This road is used to maintain White Pine Dam and also serves as the trail to the lake. Follow this road for one mile until you come to White Pine Creek and the forest service directional sign. The road to White Pine Lake branches off to the left. Follow this road for ¼ of a mile until you come to an overlook. This section of trail is much steeper than the previous mile so take a few minutes at the overlook to appreciate the views of Snowbird and to catch your breath. The hike from the overlook to the lake is uphill but is an easy hike. The scenery is spectacular and will keep you from looking at your watch on this 4½ -mile hike. Approximately ¾ of a mile from the lake you will enter a huge boulder field. The immensity of these boulders and the sheer power of the glacial ice that tossed them around like marbles will astound you. Several short switchbacks will take you through this boulder field and up over the ridge. From the ridge you will descend a couple hundred feet and a few more switchbacks to the lake.

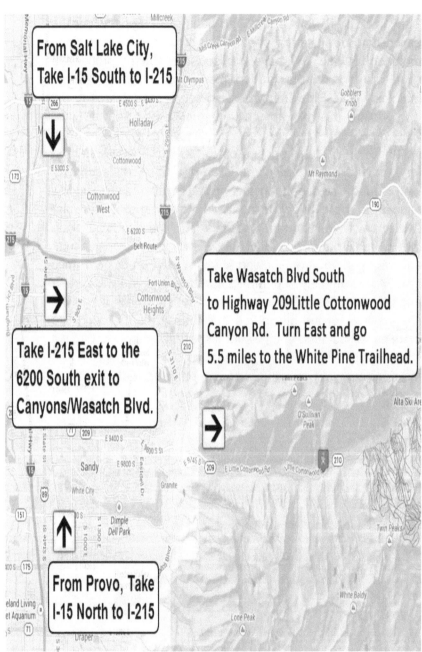

From Salt Lake City, Take I-15 South to I-215

Take I-215 East to the 6200 South exit to Canyons/Wasatch Blvd.

Take Wasatch Blvd South to Highway 209Little Cottonwood Canyon Rd. Turn East and go 5.5 miles to the White Pine Trailhead.

From Provo, Take I-15 North to I-215

Driving directions to White Pine Lake

Topography Map of White Pine Lake

167

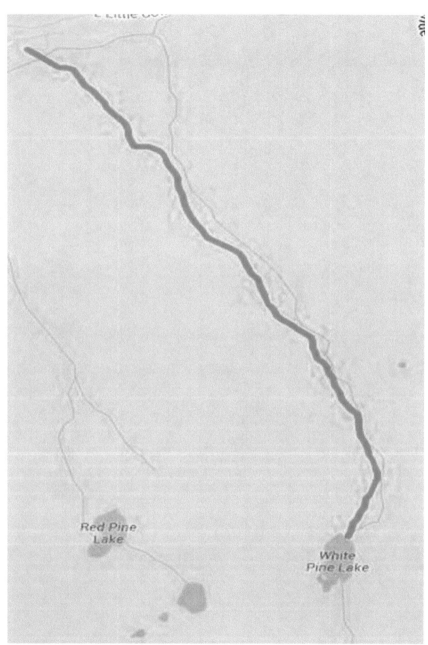

Trail Map to White Pine Lake

168

FISHING WHITE PINE LAKE:

This lake can be very productive or it can be very frustrating. Like Upper Red Pine Lake, the fish here grow big and fat. Gill net studies performed by the Department of Wildlife Resources have revealed a healthy population of Cutthroats. Many of these cutthroats were 15 inches or larger.

White Pine is a large, deep lake that can be very difficult to fish, especially when the weather is warm. During summer, the fish will concentrate near the middle of the lake or near the middle of the dam making it nearly impossible to reach them. On a summer trip I encountered such a problem. The week before the trip the weather had been unusually warm and dry. The warm weather had forced all of the fish to the deepest sections of the lake, where they were happily rising to hatches just out of reach of my best casts. I watched helplessly as the middle of the lake boiled with rising fish. Some of these fish were trophy size cutthroats in the multi-pound range. Needless to say I went home skunked that day.

Spring and fall are the best times of the year to plan a trip to this lake. The fish will be close in and easier to catch. The areas you will want to target in the spring and fall will be the stream inlet on the south side of the lake and the rocky west shoreline. Access along the west shoreline will be difficult. It is necessary to hike over many boulders to fish this section of the lake. Extreme caution should be taken especially when it is wet. Access along the east shoreline is difficult because of steep drop-offs and large boulders. Most of the fishing pressure will be concentrated on the easier access points near the stream and along the south shore.

My best success has been with jigs and metal lures. Metal lures add that extra weight needed in the summer to reach the fish in the deeper sections of the lake. The best lures will be Lil Jakes in gold with red spots, white with red spots or black with white spots. Mepps in brass and orange colors also work well on this lake.

Fly-fishing is an early morning and late evening event on this lake. Casting to rising Cutthroats in the early morning alpine light is a spectacular experience. It is also necessary. By the time the full rays of the sun are on the lake the fish are concentrated in the middle, far from even your best double haul cast. Try using a black leech pattern or Black Woolley Bugger pattern to entice the larger cutthroats.

The following map is of White Pine Lake. It is important to remember that on these high altitude lakes it could well take until the first of July for them to ice-off completely.

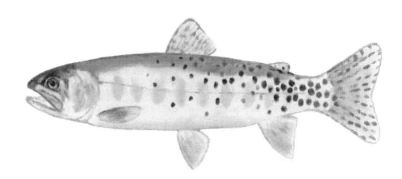

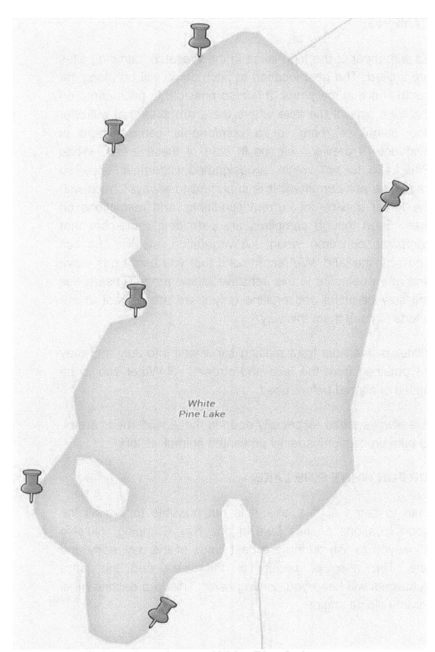

Productive fishing locations at White Pine Lake

White
Pine Lake

CAMPING:

As with most of the high lakes in the Wasatch, camping sites are limited. The best location to pitch camp will be along the south shore in the pines. It is also possible to pitch camp on the East side of the lake where there are sites that will offer you plenty of room for a comfortable camp. There is evidence of previous camps in both of these areas. White Pine Lake is not within a designated wilderness area so campfires are permitted. It is important to always check with the forest service for current conditions and restrictions on fires. Even though campfires are permitted, remember that campfires consume wood, kill vegetation, sterilize the soil and scar the land. We recommend that you use a gas stove and not a campfire in this sensitive alpine area. These areas will stay beautiful and pristine only if we are diligent in our efforts to keep them this way.

Water is available from melting snow well into July and may be obtained from the lake and stream. All Water should be boiled or filtered before used.

It is always smart, especially deep in these wilderness areas, to take precautions against unwanted animal visitors.

TIP FOR WHITE PINE LAKE:

Plan to camp at this lake. It is not possible to fish all the good locations on this lake in one day. Camping will also allow you to fish during the best times of the day, early and late. The absolute beauty of this area and the large cutthroats will keep you coming back. This is a definite must for any alpine angler.

THE LAKES RATING

A. AESTHETICS – Long but beautiful hike.

B. OUALITY OF FISHING EXPRIENCE AND FISH –Excellent for hungry pan sized Cutthroat Trout.

C. ACCESSIBILTY - Moderate

D. OVERALL RATING –EXCELLENT

UPPER BELLS CANYON RESERVOIR

ELEVATION: 10,016 feet above sea level.

ICE OFF: Ice-off generally occurs during the last week of June or the first week of July.

HIKING MILES: Approximately 9.5 miles round trip.

HIKING TIME: 5-6 hours.

WILDERNESS AREA: Lone Peak Wilderness Area.

FISH SPECIES PRESENT: Cutthroat Trout

STOCKING SCHEDULE: This lake is stocked by plane every other year. The lake has a good population of 12-14 inch cutthroat trout.

HOW TO GET THERE

The trail turn east at Lower Bells Reservoir and continues up the canyon. At about the 1.5 mile mark the trail becomes much steeper and rockier. Approximately 2. 5 miles from the trail head, you will reach Lower Upper Bells Waterfall. From the waterfall to the upper reservoir the trail gets extremely steep, rough and rocky. The trail is full of rocks and boulders that can shift and move when you step on them. Be careful on this trail. The trail is also hard to follow in spots from the waterfall to the reservoir.

One of the important things to remember when hiking this trail is that it is strenuous and can be dangerous if you are not paying attention.

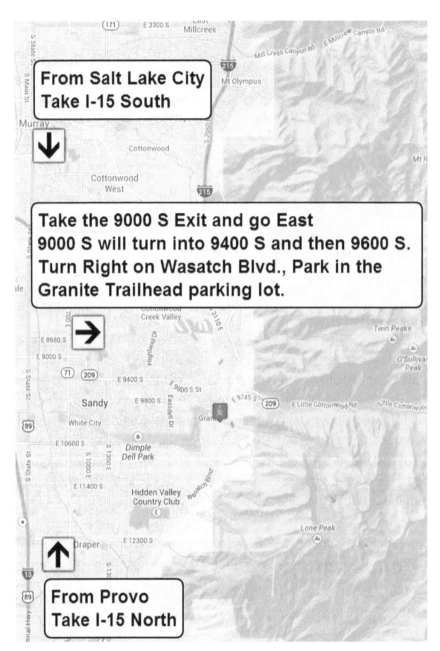

From Salt Lake City Take I-15 South

Take the 9000 S Exit and go East 9000 S will turn into 9400 S and then 9600 S. Turn Right on Wasatch Blvd., Park in the Granite Trailhead parking lot.

From Provo Take I-15 North

Driving Directions to Upper Bells Reservoir

Trail Map to Upper Bells Reservoir

177

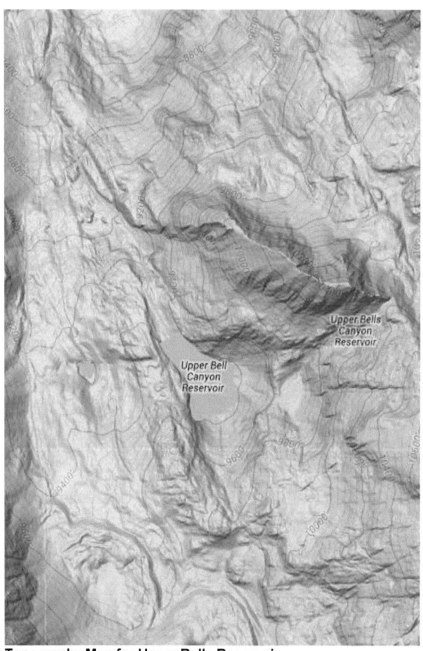

Topography Map for Upper Bells Reservoir

FISHING UPPER BELLS CANYON RESERVOIR

This lake can be very productive or it can be very frustrating depending on the level of the lake. The fishing is better in years with high water levels as the fish survive the winter much better. The lake has a good population of healthy 12-14 Cutthroat Trout.

At ice off this lake can provide some excellent fishing for hungry Cutthroat Trout. I recommend that you use mini-tube jigs in white, red and black during the first few weeks of ice off. Cast your jigs near shore structure or in the close drop off and retrieve with different jigging motions until you find the right motion to get the fish to strike. Sometimes any motion will work but at other times the fish are very picky.

During summer, the fish will concentrate near the middle of the lake. The best technique to catch fish at this lake is with metal lures and flies. During the morning and evening hours fly fishing works best. A fly and bubble cast out and retrieved slowly works well. During the heat of the day gold, silver and white Lil Jakes work the best. A gold Kastmaster also works well on the cutthroats. Cast to the middle of the reservoir and retrieve at different speeds until you find the right speed that makes the cutthroats attack the lure.

Since this lake is located at such a high elevation, the growing season for these trout is compacted into a short 2 months. The cutthroat knows this and turns the feedbag on! Even though it might be the middle of the day these fish will still strike a lure or fly if presented to them.

Spring and fall are the best times of the year to plan a trip to this lake. The fish will be hungry and easier to catch. This lake receives very little fishing pressure.

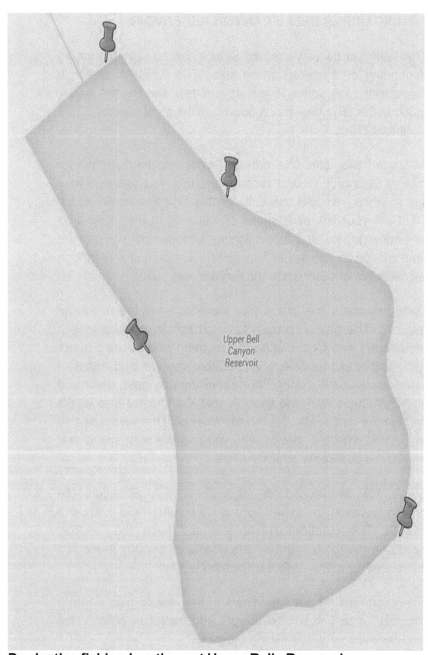

Productive fishing locations at Upper Bells Reservoir

180

CAMPING

Camping sites are limited. Remember this is a wilderness area and ground fires are prohibited. If you camp on the Southern side of the lake it will be necessary to set up camp further from the lake because of the steep slope. It is not recommended to camp on the other areas around the lake because of the steep terrain and the inability to stay far enough away from the water.

Special precautions should be made at this lake to ensure a bear free camp. Black bears do inhabit the Wasatch and can be lured into your camp by the smell of a free meal.

Water is available from melting snow well in to July and water may be taken from the lake. All water from either snow melt or the lake should be either boiled or filtered.

THE OUTDOORS GUYS RATING

A. AESTHETICS – Long but beautiful hike. This will be the toughest hike to any alpine lake in the Wasatch. However, the scenery is breathtaking and worth the extra effort.

B. OUALITY OF FISHING EXPRIENCE AND FISH –Excellent for hungry pan sized and larger Cutthroat Trout.

C. ACCESSIBILTY - Difficult

D. OVERALL RATING -Excellent

181

LOWER BELLS CANYON RESERVOIR

ELEVATION: **5580** feet above sea level.

ICE OFF: Ice-off generally occurs during last week of March or the first of April.

HIKING MILES: Approximately 1 mile.

HIKING TIME: 45 minutes.

WILDERNESS AREA: No wilderness designation, watershed area.

FISH SPECIES PRESENT: Cutthroat Trout. Catch and Release only.

STOCKING SCHEDULE: This Lake is stocked by the Utah Department of Wildlife Resources on a regular basis. Check with the Department for stocking dates.

HOW TO GET THERE

Granite Trail head - The Granite Trail head, located just east of the intersection of Wasatch Boulevard and E. Little Cottonwood Rd., provides 23 parking stalls and restrooms. The Granite Trail, which heads up to the reservoir, is a longer but not as steep trail as the Boulders Trail. The trail to the reservoir is .71 miles long and has a vertical gain of 560 ft.

Boulders Trail head - The Boulders Trail head is located .6 miles south of the intersection of Wasatch Boulevard and E. Little Cottonwood Rd. on the East side of Wasatch Boulevard, on the North side of the entrance to the Boulders at Bell Canyon housing development. The Boulders Trail head has about 20 parking stalls. The Boulders Trail up to the Lower Bell Canyon Reservoir is shorter and steeper than the Granite Trail. The trail to the reservoir from this trail head is .5 miles long and has a vertical gain of 578 ft.

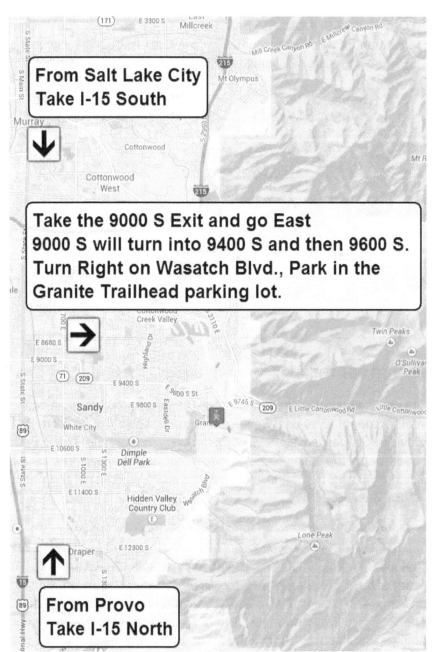

From Salt Lake City Take I-15 South

Take the 9000 S Exit and go East 9000 S will turn into 9400 S and then 9600 S. Turn Right on Wasatch Blvd., Park in the Granite Trailhead parking lot.

From Provo Take I-15 North

Driving directions to Lower Bells Reservoir

Trail Map to Lower Bells Reservoir

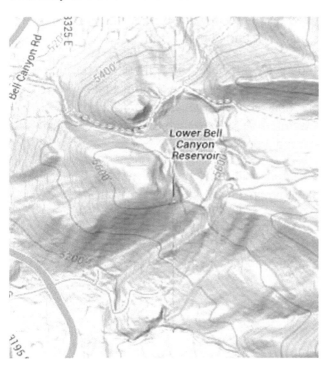

Topography Map of Lower Bells Reservoir
185

FISHING LOWER BELLS RESERVOIR

Lower Bells Reservoir is owned by the city of Sandy and is part of the Bell Canyon Nature Park. The lake has a decent population of Bonneville Cutthroat trout. The lake is stocked by the Utah Department of Wildlife resources. Since the lake has Bonneville Cutthroats in it, the state has instituted a catch and release only regulation on this lake.

This lake has some really good sized trout. It is possible to catch several 15-19+ inch trout in a day of fishing. Since it is catch and release, it is required that you use artificial flies and lures to prevent the fish from being injured or killed by swallowing a baited hook.

The best luck we have had on this reservoir has been with gold Kastmasters and gold colored Lil-Jakes. Summer evenings are a great time to take advantage of the hatches on the lake and it is possible to fly fish or use a fly and bubble combo.

In the spring, mini tube jigs work well. The fish will be cruising closer to shore and will strike a well jigged presentation. Use an assortment of colors until you find which color works best. It will depend on the day, weather and the amount of light on the lake as to what color the fish will react best to.

Spinners and other lures will work but are not as effective as Kastmaskers, Lil-Jakes or mini tube jigs.

The ice comes off early on this reservoir. The reservoir is also a popular destination for day hikers and families. If you want more elbow room and less traffic, try visiting this lake on weekdays.

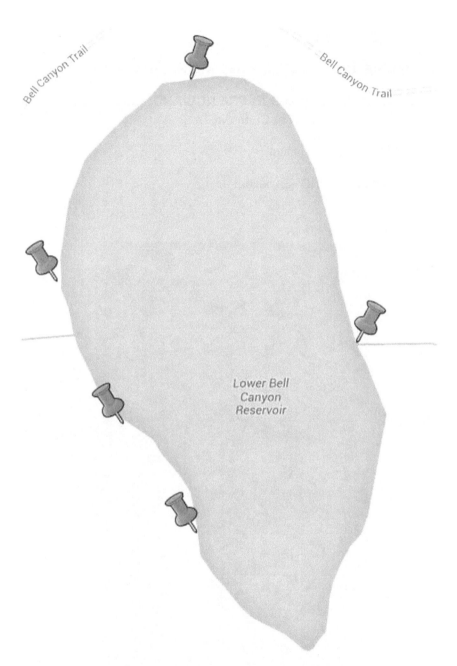

Productive fishing locations at Lower Bells Reservoir

187

THE LAKES RATING

A. AESTHETICS – Easy, quick hike. Close to homes.

B. OUALITY OF FISHING EXPRIENCE AND FISH –Excellent for hungry pan sized and larger Cutthroat Trout.

C. ACCESSIBILTY - Difficult

D. OVERALL RATING –Excellent

188

CECRET LAKE

Cecret Lake (Photo Courtesy of Eric bean)

ELEVATION: 9,750' feet above sea level.

ICE OFF: Ice-off generally occurs during the last week of June or the first week of July.

HIKING MILES: Approximately 1 mile.

HIKING TIME: 45 minutes.

WILDERNESS AREA: No wilderness designation, watershed area.

FISH SPECIES PRESENT: Lake is full of Tiger Salamanders and is not deep enough or suitable for fish.

189

HOW TO GET THERE

To get to the trail, drive up the main road of Little Cottonwood Canyon, past Alta ski resort to Albion Basin Campground. The road turns to gravel once you get past the ski resort. There's a small parking lot at the trail head. The trail crosses a footbridge over Little Cottonwood Creek and continues through spectacular wildflower meadows during late June and July and up a rocky slope to the picturesque lake. Follow the signs to avoid confusing spur trails.

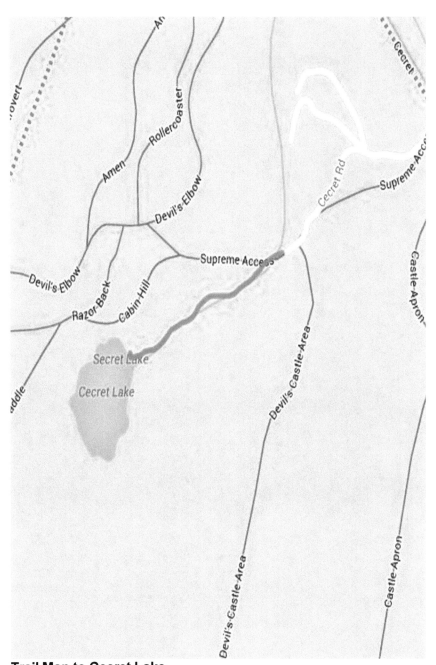

Trail Map to Cecret Lake

191

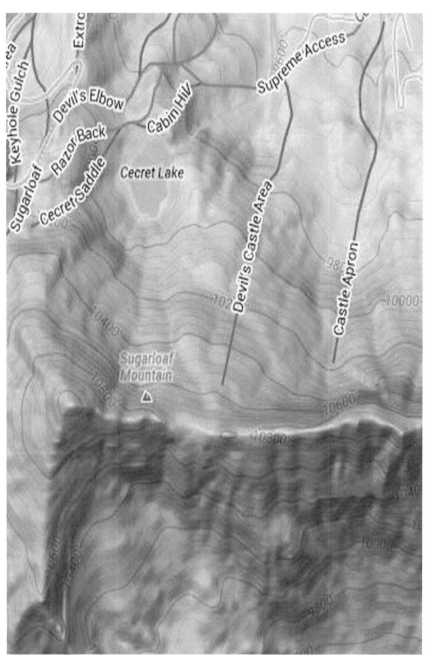

Topography Map of Cecret Lake

192

CHAPTER 8

THE LAKES OF
THE AMERICAN FORK
DRAINAGE

TIBBLE FORK RESERVOIR, SILVER FLAT RESERVOIR, SILVER LAKE, SILVER GLANCE LAKE, LAKE HARDY, PITTSBURGH LAKE

TIBBLE FORK RESERVOIR

ELEVATION: 6392' feet above sea level.

ICE OFF: Ice-off generally occurs during the first couple of weeks of March.

HIKING MILES: Park in the parking lot and walk about 100 feet.

HIKING TIME: N/A

FISH SPECIES PRESENT: Brook Trout, Rainbow Trout, some Brown and maybe a few Cutthroat Trout as well.

WILDERNESS AREA: No wilderness designation, watershed area.

STOCKING SCHEDULE:

This lake is stocked by the Utah Department of Wildlife Resources on a regular basis. Check with the Department for stocking dates.

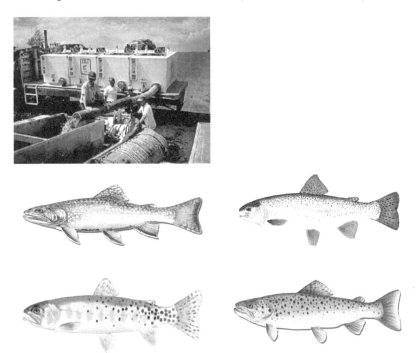

HOW TO GET THERE

From Salt Lake City, Utah, take I-15 to the Alpine-Highland exit 284. Go east on Highway 92 for 8 miles to mouth of American Fork Canyon. Go 5 miles up the canyon to junction; take the North Fork/Forest Road 85 to Tibble Fork Reservoir. Stay left on paved road for a mile to the campground.

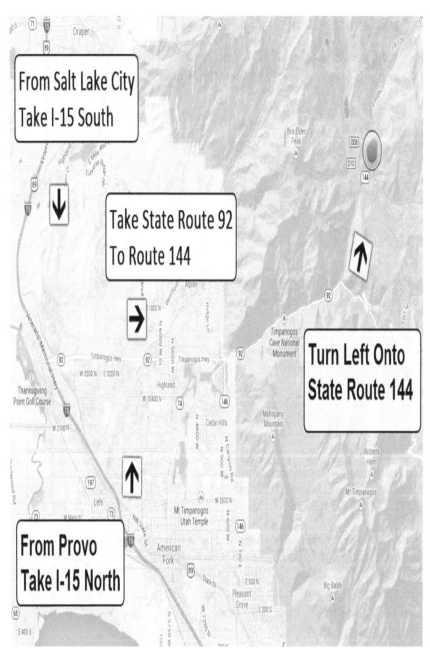

From Salt Lake City
Take I-15 South

Take State Route 92
To Route 144

Turn Left Onto
State Route 144

From Provo
Take I-15 North

Driving Directions to Tibble Fork Reservoir

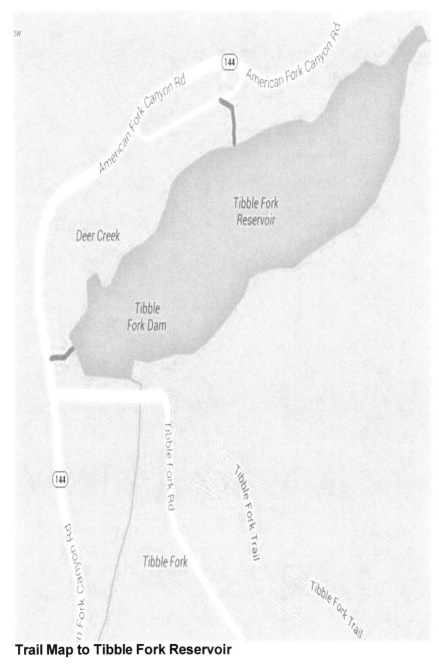

Trail Map to Tibble Fork Reservoir

197

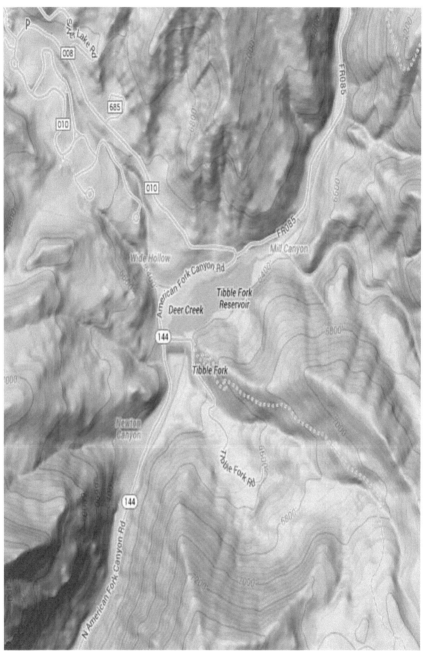

Topography Map of Tibble Fork Reservoir

FISHING TIBBLE FORK RESERVOIR

Tibble Fork Reservoir is a very popular with fishermen and gets heavy use nearly year round. During the summer the lake can be very crowded with family's picnicking and fishing. It is a great location to introduce young children to fishing. Weekends are the busiest times at this lake. If you have the ability to fish this lake during the week the crowds will be thinner.

Recently, arsenic has been discovered in high levels in the mud that is washing down from the mine tailings farther up the canyon. This mud has been accumulating in Tibble Fork Reservoir. At the time of the writing of this book, the State and Federal government are deciding how to remediate this issue at the reservoir.

The best time to fish this lake is just after ice off and in the fall. This is a great time to have some fast action on a fly or lure. Concentrate your fishing efforts on areas around the inlet stream and close to the bank. The fish will stack up near the inlet stream in the spring to snatch up food and nutrients being washed into the lake from the spring runoff. The influx of new water also replenishes the dwindled oxygen supply in the lake.

One of the most successful methods to entice both brook trout and rainbow trout in this lake is with 1/16 ounce mini-tube jig in white, red or smoke colors.

Summer fishing can be more difficult than spring or fall. In the summer when the water warms up the fish head back down to the cooler water in the deepest sections of the lake. When fishing this lake during the heat of the summer it is important to adjust your fishing methods. If possible, fish early in the morning or late in the afternoon and evening. Fly fishing during the summer can be rewarding. During the summer, hatches of May flies and midges occur and terrestrials such as grasshoppers, beetles and ants end up in the lake and on the trout's menu. Attractor patterns such as Royal Wulffs and Renegades will produce fish when no hatch is

199

present.

Lures can be just as effective during the summer months. One of the benefits of fishing with lures is that you can cast farther from the bank and into deeper water. Lures are also effective when fished from a float tube. In the summer use a #1 or #2 Lil-Jake, Crocodile, or Mepps spinner and fish them deep.

Bait fishing is also very popular and effective at this lake. Power bait, worms and worm marshmallow combinations work well on the rainbows.

The fall is another excellent time to fish this lake. The crowds will also be smaller during the fall. Brook Trout, like Brown Trout spawn in the fall. When fishing Tibble Fork in the fall concentrate on the area around the inlet stream, fish will gather near this area in anticipation of the spawn. Fly fishing to these fish can be deadly with a small egg pattern or egg sucking leach. In the fall, the fish will also frequent the near shore areas in search of food. Jigs and lures should be fished similar to spring. If you are fishing with a dry fly, concentrate on those fish that are rising. Fall fishing can be both beautiful and productive and is definitely a try.

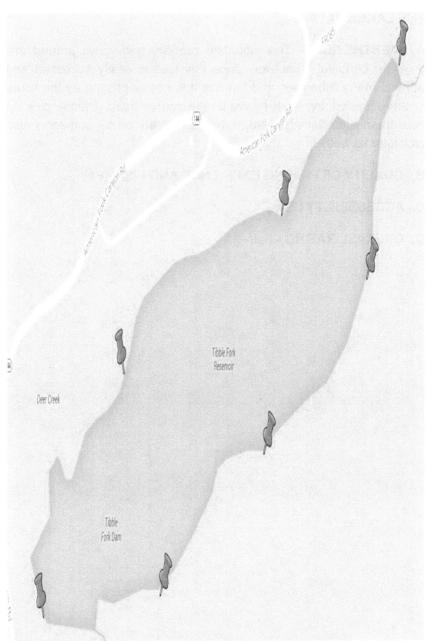

Productive fishing locations at Tibble Fork Reservoir

201

THE LAKES RATING

A. AESTHETICS – The mountain scenery and views around this lake are beautiful. However, since this lake is easily accessed and attracts many fishermen and families it is not as pristine as the lakes in the high country. With heavy usage comes trash. Please pick up your trash after fishing. Also, if you see trash left by someone else pick it up as well.

B. OUALITY OF FISHING EXPRIENCE AND FISH –Fair

C. ACCESSIBILTY - Easy

D. OVERALL RATING - Fair

SILVER LAKE FLAT RESERVOIR

Silver Lake Flat Reservoir (Photo Courtesy of Eric Bean)

ELEVATION: 7650' feet above sea level.

ICE OFF: Ice-off generally occurs during the last week of March or early April depending on spring weather conditions.

HIKING MILES: Approximately 1 mile from Tibble Fork Reservoir. Hiking to the reservoir is only needed when the road is closed.

HIKING TIME: 45 minutes.

WILDERNESS AREA: No wilderness designation, watershed area.

FISH SPECIES PRESENT: Rainbow Trout, Brook Trout

STOCKING SCHEDULE:

This lake is stocked by the Utah Department of Wildlife Resources on a regular basis. Check with the Department for stocking dates.

HOW TO GET THERE

From Salt Lake City, Utah, take I-15 to the Alpine-Highland exit 284. Go east on Highway 92 for 8 miles to mouth of American Fork Canyon. Go 5 miles up the canyon to junction; take the North Fork/Forest Road 85 to Tibble Fork Reservoir. Stay left on paved road for a mile to the lake. From the lake turn left at the sign to Granite Flats Campground and go about .8 miles to the lake.

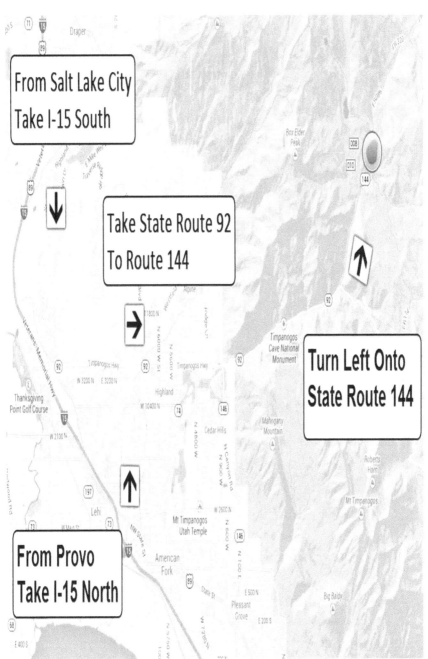

Driving directions to Silver Lake Flat Reservoir

205

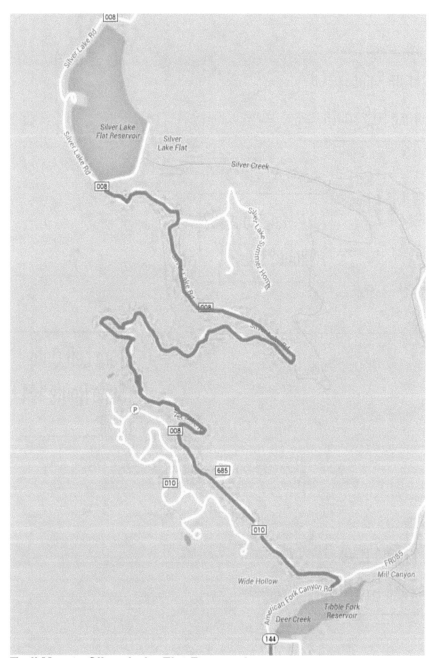

Trail Map to Silver Lake Flat Reservoir

206

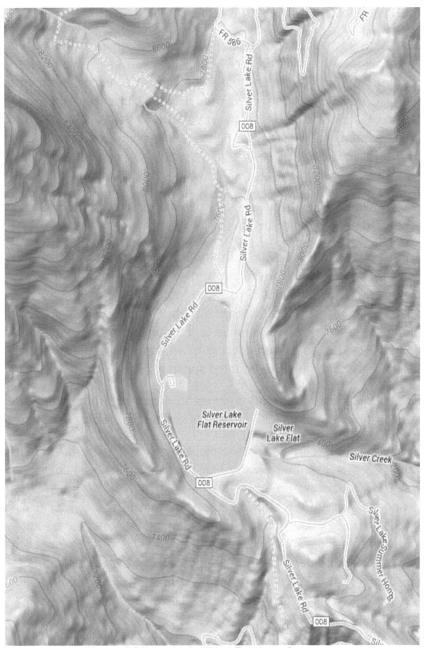

Topography Map of Silver Lake Flat Reservoir

207

FISHING SILVER FLAT RESERVOIR

Just like its neighbor Tibble Fork Reservoir, Silver Lake Flat Reservoir is also a very popular water with fishermen. This lake gets heavy use during the spring, summer and fall. During the summer the lake can be very crowded with family's picnicking and fishing. Granite Flats Campground is nearby and provides a base camp for many fishermen. Weekends are the busiest times at this lake. If you have the ability to fish this lake during the week the crowds will be thinner.

Silver Lake Flat Reservoir is a very popular rainbow trout fishery and is stocked heavily during the season.

The best time to fish Silver Lake Flat Reservoir is just after ice off. I fish this lake during the spring and have fast action on leftover rainbows and brook trout. This is a great time to have some fast action on a fly or lure. Concentrate your fishing efforts on areas around the inlet stream and close to the bank. The fish will stack up near the inlet stream in the spring to snatch up food and nutrients being washed into the lake from the spring runoff.

One of the most successful methods to entice both brook trout and rainbow trout on this lake is with a gold and red spotted Lil Jake lure.

Summer fishing can be more difficult than spring. In the summer when the water warms up the fish head back down to the cooler water in the deepest sections of the lake. When fishing this lake during the heat of the summer it is important to adjust your fishing methods. If possible, fish early in the morning or late in the afternoon and evening. Also, try using a float tube to fish the deeper sections of this lake. Lures and bait are the most effective methods during the summer months. Lures are also effective when fished from a float tube. In the summer use a #1 or #2 Lil-Jake, Crocodile, or Mepps spinner and fish them deep.

Bait fishing is also very popular and effective at this lake. Power bait, worms and worm marshmallow combinations work well on the rainbows.

The fall is another excellent time to fish this lake. The crowds will also be smaller during the fall. The Brook Trout will try to spawn in the fall and the rainbows will be gorging themselves getting ready for winter.

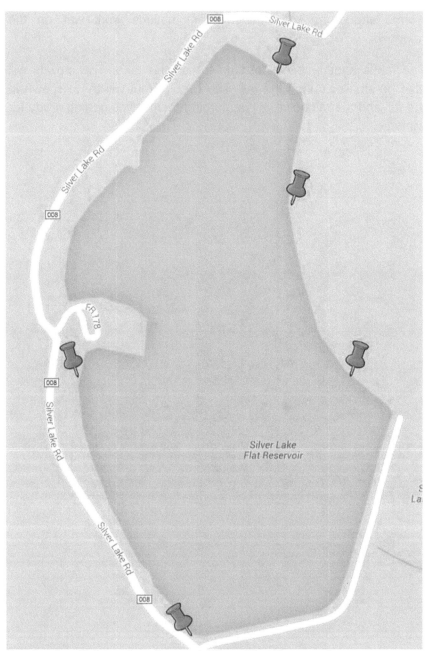

Productive fishing locations at Silver Flat Reservoir

SILVER LAKE

(AMERICAN FORK CANYON)

Silver Lake (Photo Courtesy of Eric Bean)

ELEVATION: 9000 feet above sea level.

ICE OFF: Silver Lake takes longer to ice off than other lakes at a similar elevation. This is due in large part to the cirque that blocks the sun and prolongs ice off. The ice is usually off around the first week in June.

HIKING MILES: 1 3/4 MILES.

HIKING TIME: 1 1/2 HOURS.

AVERAGE SIZE OF FISH: Silver Lake contains some of the largest and fattest Brook trout in the Wasatch. Silver Lake currently shows

211

no sign of over population. The average size of fish in this lake range from 11 to 12 inches with larger 13 to 15 inch fish possible.

WILDERNESS AREA: Lone Peak Wilderness Area.

FISHING USAGE: Weekdays - Light, weekends - Moderate.

FISH SPECIES PRESENT: Brook Trout, Arctic Grayling

STOCKING SCHEDULE: This Lake is stocked by plane every other year. Check with the Division of Wild Life Resources for exact schedule.

HOW TO GET THERE:

Silver Lake is located within the boundaries of the Uinta National Forest and the Lone Peak wilderness. The lake is situated in a picturesque cirque at the base of 11, 321 foot White Baldy peek. The trail head is 11.8 miles from the mouth of American Fork canyon and is located at the West end of Silver Flat Reservoir. To get to silver Flat Reservoir, begin at the mouth of the canyon on Route 92, go east on 92 past Timpanogos Cave National Monument, Hanging Rock picnic area (closed), North Mill and Little mill Campgrounds and turn left on route 085. Follow route 085 to the north end of Tibble Fork Reservoir. The road will fork; stay on the paved road to the Granite Flat Campground entrance. Just before the campground gate turn left onto a dirt road. Follow this dirt road for just over three miles to the parking area at the north end of Silver Flat Reservoir. Bathroom facilities are located at the start of the trail.

The trail, heads north through aspen trees and alongside the stream for about a 1/4 of a mile. The trail turns west and you enter the Lone peak Wilderness, from here you continue west until you get to some small cliffs. The trail turns north and you cross a small stream on a log bridge. The trail then ascends the oak- covered ridge on a single switch back. As you near the top of this first ridge you will cross an old mine tailings pile, stop and take in the incredible view of the Wasatch Mountains and Silver Flat reservoir. The trail continues west with a small stream and meadow area on your left and the ridge on your right. As you near the next set of small cliffs you will switch back up the ridge and once again a small stream and meadow area will be on your left. Follow the trail until you reach the Lake. During heavy snow years the last section of this trail can be covered in snow until the first of June. Make sure of your footing to prevent injuries from falling through rotting ice and wedging your foot in the numerous rocks below the snow.

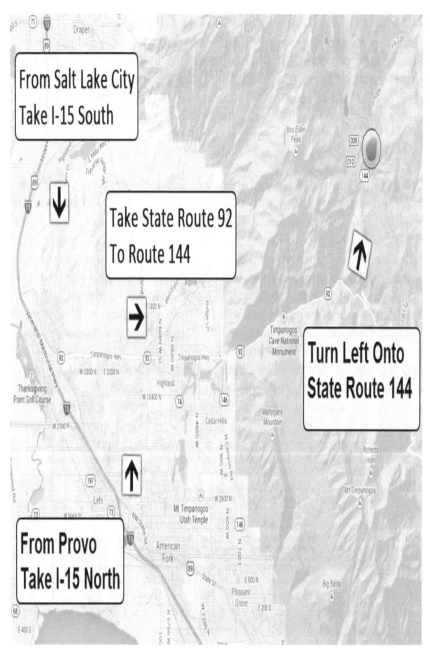

Driving directions to Silver Lake "American Fork Canyon"

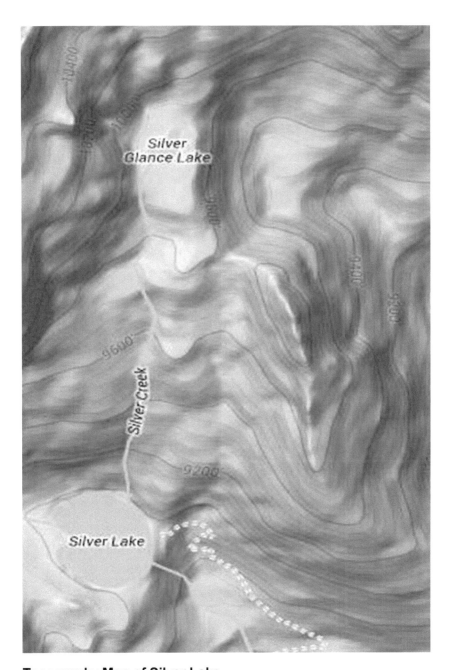

Topography Map of Silver Lake

215

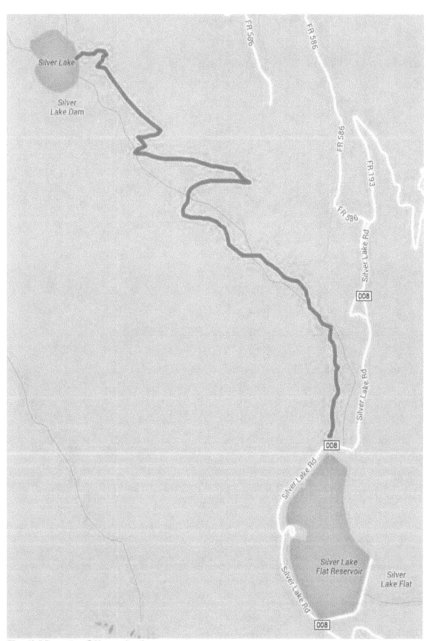

Trail Map to Silver Lake

216

FISHING SILVER LAKE:

The best time to fish this lake is at Ice off. The toughest challenge is timing the precise moment that enough ice has come off the lake. This is important and can mean the difference between catching fish and just fishing. It has been my experience with this lake that the water needs to warm to a sufficient temperature before the fish begin to feed in earnest. Don't jump the gun and hike to this lake before it has relinquished most of its ice cap. I have trekked to this lake many times in anticipation of an Ice free body of water only to find it 90 to 95 percent covered in ice. It is easy to make this mistake, especially in May when the valley temperatures are hovering near eighty and the hills are as green as Ireland.

My best success has been when the lake is at least 50 percent ice-free. As the ice retreats, concentrate on the east shoreline and the Northwest corner of the lake. These areas ice off early and tend to provide the first fishing successes. It is best to work the shoreline near rocks, dead fall and submerged willows. At the northwest corner of the lake there is a large rock which is near the inlet stream. It is possible to climb on this rock and see cruising brook trout in the water below. This is a good location, especially early in the year to catch large Brookies. Be careful when crossing the far- west side of the lake which is protected by the large cirque. The snow is deep, weak and rotting from the ground up and all it takes is one wrong step to ruin your whole year.

A couple of years ago. The Division of Wildlife Resources fixed the old manmade dam. It was allowing too much water to leave the lake and the lake was susceptible to winter kill and the low water conditions were not conducive to producing large fish. Since the dam has been fixed the water level in the lake stays constant and has allowed the fish to stay health and grow larger.

The Division of Wildlife Resources has also stocked this lake with arctic grayling! This is great news and the fish are surviving well.

217

The arctic grayling is not native to Utah, but it has been introduced into several high elevation lakes in the Uinta Mountains and now into the Wasatch.

The arctic grayling eats primarily invertebrates, including insects, insect larvae, and zooplankton. The species spawns in streams during the early spring, and eggs hatch in two to three weeks. Arctic grayling prefer clear cold water and the species does best in streams and lakes containing at least some aquatic vegetation. Grayling can live and reproduce in lakes that are marginal for trout because of low dissolved oxygen levels in winter.

Grayling are related to trout and can be caught using familiar techniques. Small lures and small, dark flies are usually effective as well as mini-tube jigs.

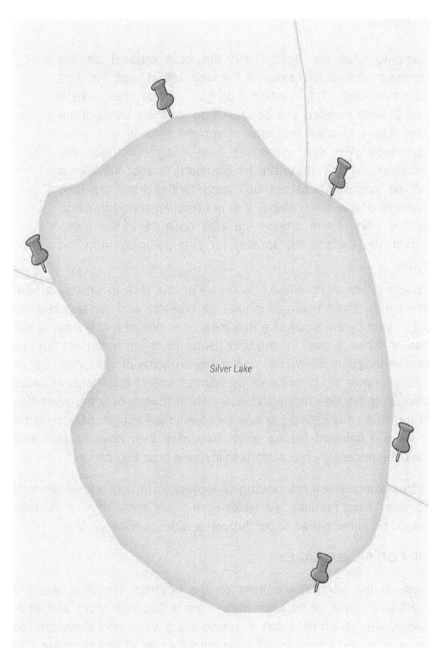

Productive fishing locations at Silver Lake

CAMPING:

Camping sites are limited and are best situated on the southern and eastern sides of the lake and at least 200 feet from the water. The Eastern side has several areas where people have camped and does provide excellent views of the lake. There is also evidence of ground fires in this area. Remember this is a wilderness area and ground fires are prohibited. If you camp on the Southern side of the lake it will be necessary to set up camp further from the lake because of the steep slope. It is not recommended to camp on the other areas around the lake because of the steep terrain and the inability to stay far enough away from the water.

Special precautions should be made at this lake to ensure a bear free camp. Black bears do inhabit the Wasatch and can be lured into your camp by the smell of a free meal. It is indeed a rare treat to see one of these bears in the wild. Because these animals are so elusive they are referred to as the black ghosts of the forest. On an early summer trip to this lake we witness one of these elusive bears traversing the side of the mountain which towers over the west side of the lake. It is exciting to see these animals from a distance but it is quite a different feeling when they stick their nose in your tent! Take the necessary precautions to insure a bear free camp.

Water is available from melting snow well in to July and water may be taken from the lake. All water from either snow melt or the lake should be either boiled or put through a water purification filter.

TIP FOR SILVER LAKE:

Early in the year, concentrate on the northern shoreline and the northwest corner of the lake. Make sure to fish near rocks and other underwater structure. Don't overlook areas you might think are too close to shore; I have caught fish within a foot of the shoreline. Try several jigs, lures and flies until you find the right pattern. Fish this

220

lake for the arctic grayling.

THE LAKE RATING

A. AESTHETICS: Long beautiful hike. Lots of animal watching opportunities.

B. ACCESSIBILITY: Moderate hike. The lake has very good access along the shoreline.

C. OVERALL RATING. Very Good

SILVER GLANCE LAKE

Silver Glance Lake (Photo Courtesy of Eric Bean)

ELEVATION: 9,805' feet above sea level.

ICE OFF: Ice-off generally occurs during the first week of July.

HIKING MILES: Approximately 1 mile.

HIKING TIME: 45 minutes.

WILDERNESS AREA: Lone Peak Wilderness Area.

FISH SPECIES PRESENT: Lake is full of Tiger Salamanders and is not deep enough or suitable for fish. The lake use to be stocked with arctic grayling but due to bad water conditions the fish did not survive.

HOW TO GET THERE:

Silver Glance Lake is located within the boundaries of the Uinta National Forest and the Lone Peak wilderness. The lake is situated above Silver Lake.

The trail head is located 11.5 miles up American Fork canyon and is located at the West end of Silver Flat Reservoir. To get to silver Flat Reservoir, begin at the mouth of the canyon on Route 92, go east on 92 past Timpanogos Cave National Monument, Hanging Rock picnic area (closed), North Mill and Little mill Campgrounds and turn left on route 085. Follow route 085 to the north end of Tibble Fork Reservoir. The road will fork; stay on the paved road to the Granite Flat Campground entrance. Just before the campground gate turn left onto a dirt road. Follow this dirt road for just over three miles to the parking area at the north end of Silver Flat Reservoir. Bathroom facilities are located at the start of the trail.

The trail, heads north through aspen trees and alongside the stream for about a 1/4 of a mile. The trail turns west and you enter the Lone peak Wilderness, from here you continue west until you get to some

223

small cliffs. The trail turns north and you cross a small stream on a log bridge. The trail then ascends the oak- covered ridge on a single switch back. As you near the top of this first ridge you will cross an old mine tailings pile, stop and take in the incredible view of the Wasatch Mountains and Silver Flat reservoir. The trail continues west with a small stream and meadow area on your left and the ridge on your right. As you near the next set of small cliffs you will switch back up the ridge and once again a small stream and meadow area will be on your left. Follow the trail until you reach Silver Lake. From Silver Lake the trail to Silver Glance Lake will be located at the North end of Silver Lake. During heavy snow years the last section of this trail can be covered in snow until the first of June. Make sure of your footing to prevent injuries from falling through rotting ice and wedging your foot in the numerous rocks below the snow.

View of Silver Glance, Silver Lake and Silver Lake Flat Reservoir

(Photo Courtesy of Eric Bean)

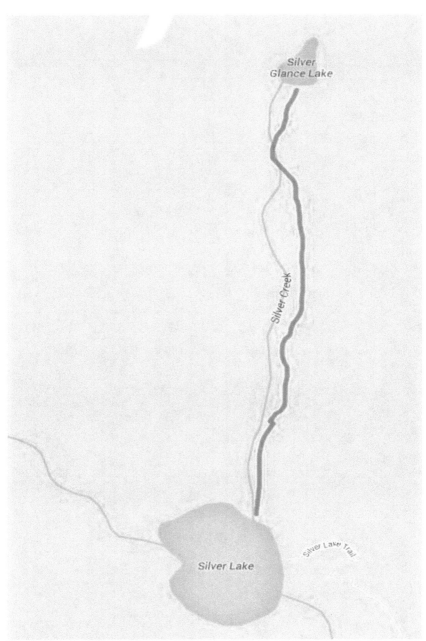

Trail Map to Silver Glance Lake

225

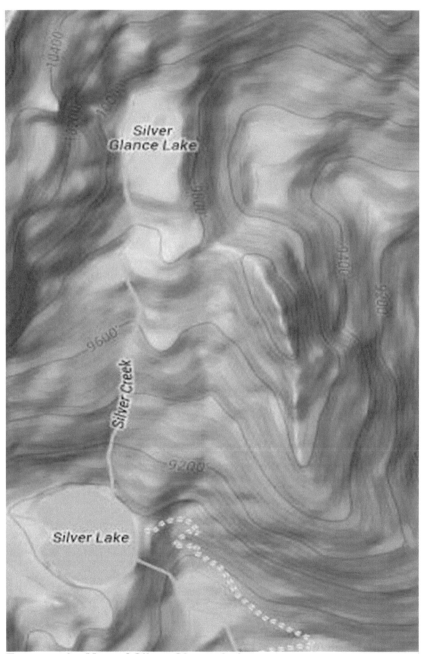

Topography Map of Silver Glance Lake

PITTSBURGH LAKE

ELEVATION: 9,750' feet above sea level.

ICE OFF: Ice-off generally occur during the last week of June or the first week of July.

HIKING MILES: Approximately 1 mile.

HIKING TIME: 45 minutes.

WILDERNESS AREA: No wilderness designation, watershed area.

FISH SPECIES PRESENT: Lake is full of Brook Trout.

STOCKING SCHEDULE: This lake is stocked by plane every other year. Check with the Division of Wild Life Resources for exact schedule.

HOW TO GET HERE:

From Salt Lake City, Utah, take I-15 to the Alpine-Highland exit 284. From Provo City, take I-15 North to exit 284. Get off I-15 at exit 284 and go east on Highway 92 for 8 miles to mouth of American Fork Canyon. Go 5 miles up the canyon to junction; take the North Fork/Forest Road 85 to Tibble Fork Reservoir. At the East end of Tibble Fork Reservoir will be a dirt road that will take you to Pittsburgh Lake. Stay to the right on this dirt road until you reach the Pittsburgh Lake Trail Head.

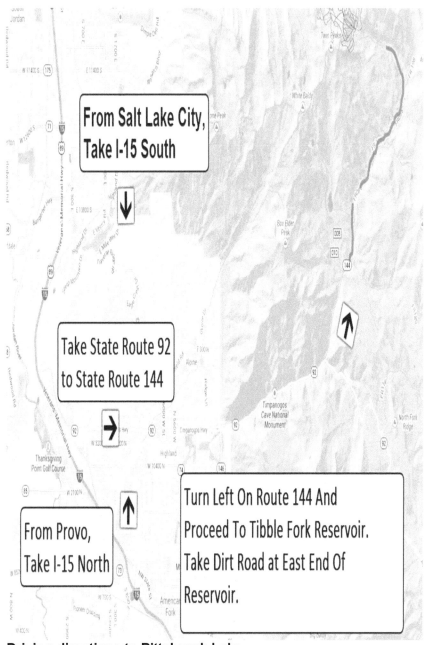

From Salt Lake City, Take I-15 South

Take State Route 92 to State Route 144

From Provo, Take I-15 North

Turn Left On Route 144 And Proceed To Tibble Fork Reservoir. Take Dirt Road at East End Of Reservoir.

Driving directions to Pittsburgh Lake

229

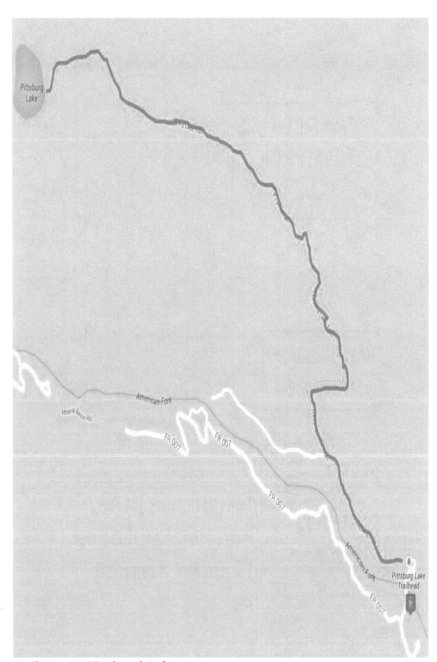

Trail Map to Pittsburgh Lake

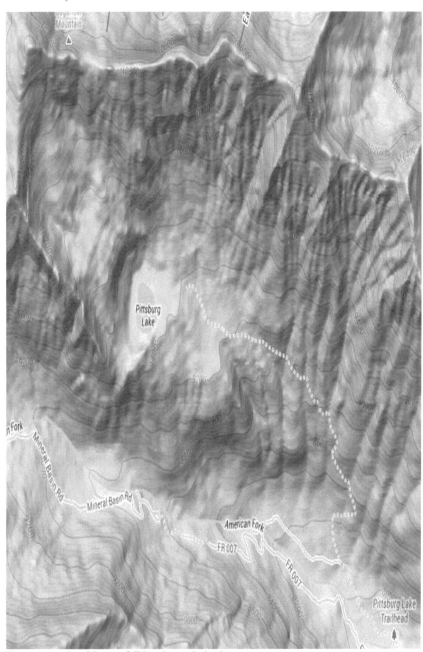

Topography Map of Pittsburgh Lake

231

FISHING PITTSBURGH LAKE:

Like most of the Alpine lakes in this region, the best time to fish this lake is at Ice off. The toughest challenge is timing the precise moment that enough ice has come off the lake. This is important and can mean the difference between catching fish and just fishing.

The hike to this lake is a constant incline and will take you at least 2-3 hours to reach the lake. Once at the lake, the best success has been when the lake is ice free. Concentrate on the east shoreline and the Northwest corner of the lake.

This lake is full of brook trout. On a recent trip to this lake, the water looked like it was boiling with thousands of brook trout feeding on the surface. It is best to work the shoreline near rocks, dead fall and submerged Structure. At the south east corner of the lake is an old homesteader's cabin. This is an interesting piece of history to explore.

The best tackle for this lake has been mini tube jigs in white, black and gray speckled and red. Small spinners and Mepps also work well on this lake. Fly fishing this lake when the hatch is on can be an exhilarating experience. The only problem with fly fishing on this lake is the casting hazards. It is recommended that you use a roll cast on this lake to avoid the trees and other casting hazards. Attractor patterns such as Royal Wulffs, Renegades and hopper imitations work well.

As you will notice when you reach the lake, you will see thousands of fish swimming around in the lake. It is important that you keep your limit of fish at this lake. Fishermen should take their limit of trout home with them at this lake since it will help decrease the population of small brook trout and allow more food for the other trout to grow larger.

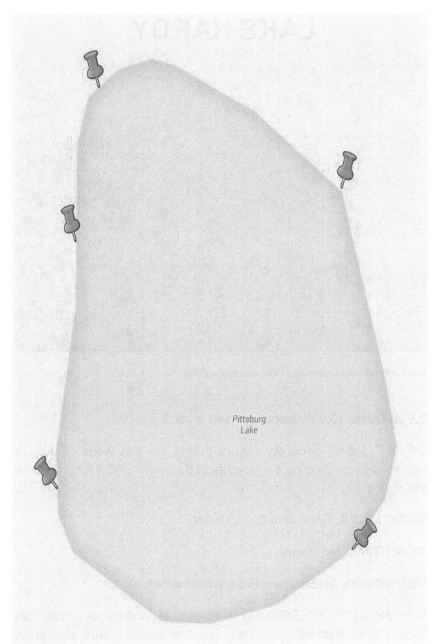

Productive fishing locations at Pittsburgh Lake

LAKE HARDY

Lake Lillian (Photo Courtesy of WasatchHiker.com)

ELEVATION: 10,035' feet above sea level.

ICE OFF: Ice-off generally occurs during the first week of July or even later depending on the severity of the winter and if it has been a cool spring...

HIKING MILES: Approximately 10 miles.

HIKING TIME: 6-8 hours.

WILDERNESS AREA: Lone Peak Wilderness Area.

FISH SPECIES PRESENT: The division of wildlife resources has tried to stock this lake with fish. The last stocking was with arctic grayling by plane. All of the fish have died and it appears to be an oxygen issue and no fish survived. There are also no Tiger Salamanders in this lake.

HOW TO GET THERE

Beginning SR-92, turn north on to 4800 W (Canyon Crest Rd). At the traffic circle, take the 1st exit onto Main St, then turn right onto Center St. Take the 2nd left onto 200 E St, and then turn left onto Alpine Cove Dr. Take the 2nd left onto Aspen Dr, and then take a right onto the dirt road. Parking for the trail is available near the Lehi city gate. Please park in a manner that does not block the road, gate, or utility operations. Hike on dirt road for approx. 2 miles until trail head.   Access this trail from the North Mountain trail #046.

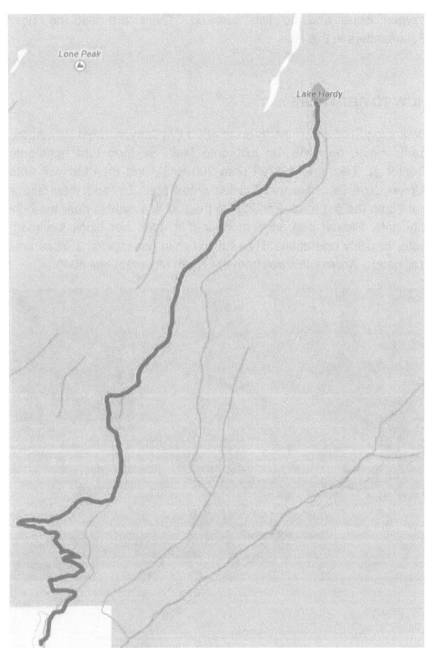

Trail Map to Lake Hardy

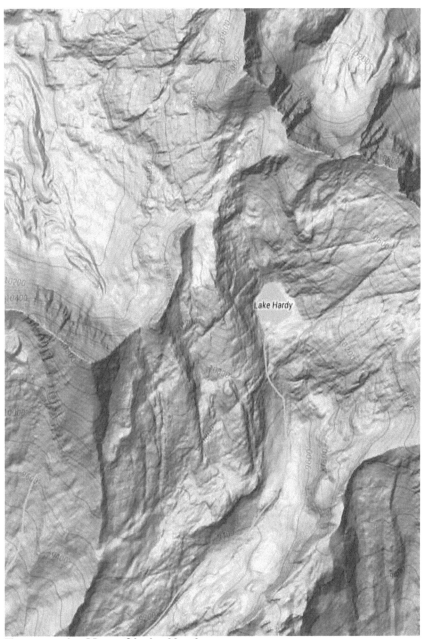

Topography Map of Lake Hardy

237

CHAPTER 9

THE LAKES OF GUARDSMAN PASS/BONANZA FLAT

LACKAWAXEN LAKE, BLOODS LAKE, LAKE BRIMHALL, SILVER LAKE ISLET

LACKAWAXEN LAKE

Lake Lackawaxen (Photo courtesy of Melinda Wickham)

ELEVATION: 10,000 feet above sea level.

ICE OFF: Ice-off generally occurs during the first week of July or even later depending on the severity of the winter and if it has been a cool spring...

HIKING MILES: Approximately 4 miles

HIKING TIME: 2-3 hours

WILDERNESS AREA: No wilderness designation.

FISH SPECIES PRESENT: The division of wildlife resources has tried to stock this lake with fish in the 90's but the lake frequently winter kills and they stopped the stocking program. The last stocking was with cutthroats by plane. While it is possible that a few fish may have survived it is highly unlikely

HOW TO GET THERE

Drive up Big Cottonwood Canyon road until you get to the sign for Guardsman Pass. Turn at that road and follow to the Guardsman Pass summit. The trail to the lake begins at Guardsman Summit and is approximately 4 miles round trip. The trail is scenic and is not a very difficult trail to hike. There are a couple of steep sections to this trail but take your time and you should have no issues.

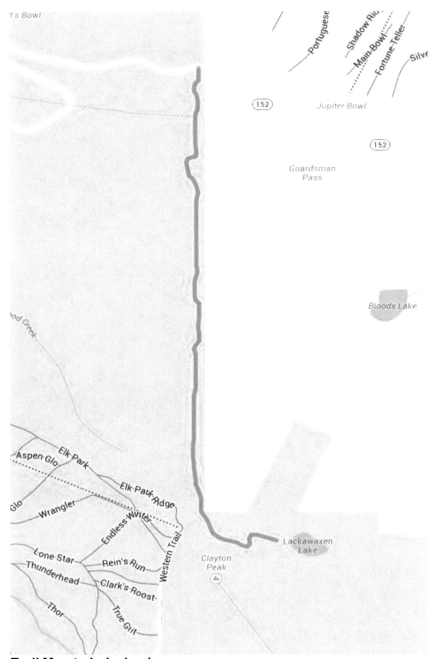

Trail Map to Lake Lackawaxen

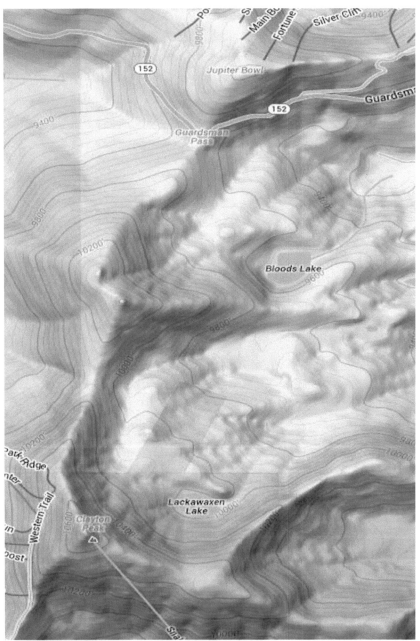

Topograhy Map of Lake Lackawaxen

BLOODS LAKE

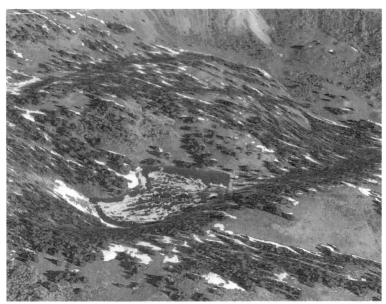

ELEVATION: 10,000 feet above sea level.

ICE OFF: Ice-off generally occurs during the first week of July or even later depending on the severity of the winter and if it has been a cool spring...

HIKING MILES: Private Property

HIKING TIME: 2-3 hours

WILDERNESS AREA: No wilderness designation.

FISH SPECIES PRESENT: The division of wildlife resources has no record of stocking this lake. You have to pass through private land to get to the lake and the lake may be privately owned.

HOW TO GET THERE: Private Property

LAKE BRIMHALL

ELEVATION: 9144 feet above sea level.

ICE OFF: Ice-off generally occurs during the first week of July or even later depending on the severity of the winter and if it has been a cool spring...

244

HIKING MILES: Private Property

HIKING TIME: Private Property

WILDERNESS AREA: No wilderness designation.

FISH SPECIES PRESENT: Since this property is privately owned by the Girl Scouts of America, the Division of Wildlife Resources has no authority or responsibility to stock this lake.

HOW TO GET THERE: Private Property

SILVER LAKE ISLET

ELEVATION: 9104 feet above sea level.

ICE OFF: Ice-off generally occurs during the last week of June or the first week of July depending on the severity of the winter and if it has been a cool spring.

HIKING MILES: Private Property

HIKING TIME: Private Property

WILDERNESS AREA: No wilderness designation, watershed area.

FISH SPECIES PRESENT: Possible population of Cutthroat

HOW TO GET THERE: Private Property

CHAPTER 10
LAKES OF THE PARLEYS CANYON

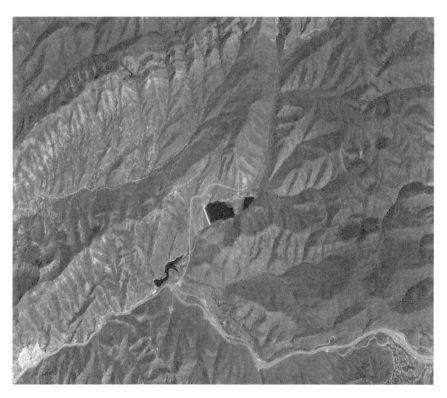

**LITTLE DELL RESERVOIR,
MOUNTAIN DELL RESERVOIR**

LITTLE DELL
RESERVOIR

ELEVATION: 5798 feet **above sea level.**

Surface Area: 249 acres

Depth: 200.1 ft

Avg. Depth: 82.4 ft.

ICE OFF: Ice-off generally occurs early on this reservoir and can happen as early as mid-March depending of the severity of the winter.

HIKING MILES: Drive to lake.

HIKING TIME: N/A

WILDERNESS AREA: No wilderness designation, watershed area.

FISH SPECIES PRESENT: Cutthroat and Brook Trout

STOCKING SCHEDULE: This lake is stocked by the Utah Division of Wildlife Resources. Check with the Division of Wild Life Resources for exact schedule.

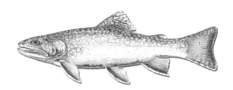

Special Regulations: Little Dell Reservoir is **CLOSED** to the possession of Cutthroat Trout. All Cutthroat Trout caught must be immediately released. **Artificial Flies and Lures only.**

The reservoir is open during daylight hours only from April 1- October 31. Fishing from a boat with a motor is illegal

HOW TO GET THERE:

Take I-80 East from the base of Parleys Canyon 5.3 miles to exit 134 UT-65 N toward East Canyon. Take UT-65 2.9 miles to the reservoir parking.

Driving Directions to Little Dell Reservoir

251

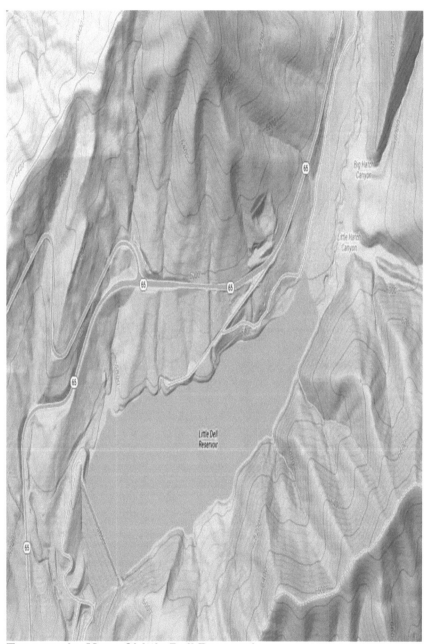

Topography Map of Little Dell Reservoir

FISHING LITTLE DELL RESERVOIR:

Little Dell Reservoir is close to the city yet it is not heavily fished. This is probably due to the artificial flies and lures requirement and you have to release all cutthroats. It is a quiet spot to fish mid week and a great place to fly fish in the fall.

The best times to fish Little Dell Reservoir are in the spring and again in the fall.

During the spring, concentrate your fishing efforts on areas around the inlet stream and close to the bank. The fish will stack up near the inlet stream in the spring to snatch up food and nutrients being washed into the lake from the spring runoff and the cutthroats will be starting to spawn.

In the fall, fishing for cutthroats, browns and brook trout will be fast pretty much everywhere around the reservoir. The fish will be feeding heavily to get prepared for the upcoming winter. Also, the level of the reservoir will be lower as the reservoir is used as a source for Salt Lake culinary water.

Fly fishermen should use attractor patterns on top and brightly colored streamer patterns or dark leech patterns below the water.

Summer fishing can be more difficult than spring or fall. In the summer when the water warms up the fish head back down to the cooler water in the deepest sections of the lake. When fishing this lake during the heat of the summer it is important to adjust your fishing methods. If possible, fish early in the morning or late in the afternoon and evening. The best time to fish during the summer is in the evenings when the hatch is coming off the lake. Lures and bait are the most effective methods during the summer months. In the summer use a #1 or #2 Lil-Jake, Crocodile, or Mepps spinner and fish them deep. Copper, gold, black and orange spoons and lures also work well on this reservoir.

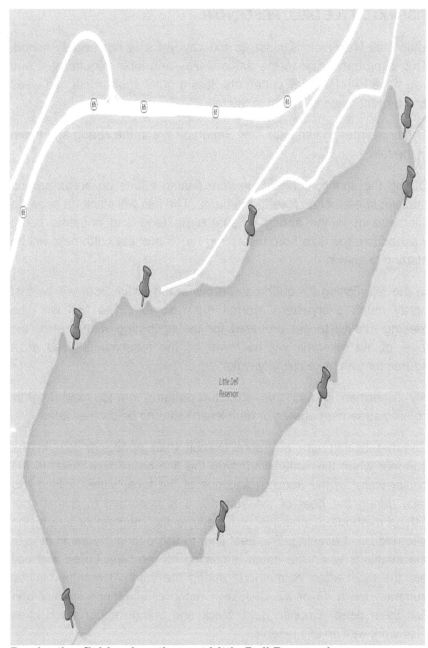

Productive fishing locations at Little Dell Reservoir

MOUNTAIN DELL RESERVOIR

ELEVATION: 9104 feet above sea level.

Closed to fishing

CHAPTER 11
SAFETY IN THE WASATCH

"PREPARDENESS IS KEY TO A SAFE TRIP"

The Wasatch Mountains are not a local park. Playing in these mountains has an inherit danger associated with them, especially if you are not prepared or are careless. Every year, people get injured, lost or even killed in these mountains. Nearly all of the time the reason is because they were not prepared for an incident. Sudden changes in weather, careless footing, going off trail and just a lack of common sense can lead to a catastrophe.

It is also important that you recognize that the animals in the Wasatch are not tame and the area is not a zoo. These animals are wild and some of them can seriously injure or kill you. It is very rare to be attacked by an animal but it can happen. Nearly every time someone has a negative encounter with an animal it is because the person got to close or tried to feed them. Please use common sense when you encounter any of the creatures that live in the Wasatch. Give the plenty of space and give them the respect they are due. Remember, you are a guest in their home.

The following information was obtained from both the US Forest Service website and the Utah Division of Wildlife resources.

BEAR SAFETY

Bears often live in the same places we camp, hike and build our houses. This poses a safety concern for both humans and bears. If a bear obtains food from a home or campsite — even once — it may become aggressive in future attempts. This almost guarantees the bear will have to be destroyed. Fortunately, there are steps you can take to protect both you and the bear.

Camp and hike responsibly

Sloppy campers and hikers don't just endanger themselves, but also future visitors. Bears have amazing memories; they will return to a site repeatedly if they ate there at some point in the past. When in bear country, you should: **Maintain a bear-safe campsite**

Store food, drinks and scented items securely (in your vehicle, a bear-safe container or a tree — never in your tent)

Dispose of trash in bear-proof dumpsters, if available

Wipe down picnic tables

Burn food off stoves or grills

Pitch tents away from trails in the backcountry

Always sleep inside your tent

Never approach or feed a bear

Report bear sightings to your campground host

Take precautions while hiking

Stay alert at dawn and dusk, when bears are more active

Go with a group, if possible

258

Make noise as you travel through dense cover

Stay away from animal carcasses

Store food, trash and scented items (such as sunscreen) in airtight plastic bags

Keep kids in the center of the group

If you encounter a bear

Stand your ground. Never back up, lie down or play dead. Stay calm and give the bear a chance to leave. Prepare to use your bear spray or another deterrent.

Don't run away or climb a tree. Black bears are excellent climbers and can run up to 35 mph — you cannot out climb or outrun them.

Know bear behavior. If a bear stands up, grunts, moans or makes other sounds, it's not being aggressive. These are the ways a bear gets a better look or smell and expresses its interest.

If a bear attacks

Use bear spray. Then leave the area. Studies have shown bear spray to be 92 percent successful in deterring bear attacks.

Shoot to kill. If you use a firearm, never fire a warning shot — aim for the center of the bear and keep firing until it is dead. Notify the Division of Wildlife Resources immediately.

Always fight back. And never give up! People have successfully defended themselves with almost anything: rocks, sticks, backpacks, water bottles and even their hands and feet.

COUGAR SAFETY

Photo courtesy of the Utah Division of Wildlife Resources

What to do if you meet an aggressive cougar. Cougars are exciting animals to see in the wild and rarely cause problems for humans. Although unlikely to happen, you should know how to react if you encounter an aggressive cougar:

Do not run from a cougar. Running will provoke an instinctive prey response and the cougar may pursue you.

Make yourself look intimidating. Make eye contact with the cougar, which cougars consider a threat. Make yourself look big by opening your jacket, raising your arms and waving them. Speak loud and firm to the cougar.

If you have children, pick them up. Try to pick children up before they panic and run. When you are picking children up, keep eye contact with the cougar and try not to bend over too far or turn your back to the cougar.

If you are attacked, fight back! Protect your head and neck, as the neck is the target for the cougar. If the cougar thinks it is not likely to win its fight with you quickly, it will probably give up and leave.

Facts about cougars

The cougar is also known as the mountain lion, puma or panther.

The cougar is one of North America's largest cats and is recognized by its tawny color and long tail.

Cougar kittens, or cubs, have blackish-brown spots on their body and dark rings on their tails that fade as they get older.

Cougars are solitary animals, making them a rare sight for humans. They usually hunt alone and at night, ambushing their prey from behind. Typically, cougars kill their prey with a bite to the lower neck.

After making a kill, a cougar often will take the carcass to the base of a tree and cover it with dirt, leaves or snow, saving it to eat later.

Cougars live all across Utah, from high in the Uinta Mountains to the dry southern Utah deserts.

Cougars' main prey is deer, so cougars are often found close to deer.

Cougars live up to 12 years in the wild but have lived up to 25 years in captivity. In the wild they face death through accidents, disease and large predators (including humans).

Playing in cougar country

If you recreate in cougar country, here are a few guidelines to make your experience safer:

Hike with other people and make noise. Cougars usually will not bother groups of people.

Keep a clean camp and store food and garbage in your vehicle or hang it between two trees where cougars (and bears) cannot reach it.

When hiking with small children, keep the children in the group or in sight ahead of the group. Remember, cougars ambush from behind, so keeping a child in front of the main group will lessen the possibility of attack.

Keep away from dead animals, especially deer or elk. This could be a kill that a cougar is guarding or will be returning to. A cougar will defend its food.

If hiking with pets, keep them close to the group. Roaming pets will be open to cougar attacks or could irritate a cougar that is trying to avoid the group.

SAFETY PRECAUTIONS

The following information is directly from the United States Forest Service Website regarding safety in the back country. It is very important that before heading out to one of these Wasatch lakes that you read understand and implement these safety precautions into your plans;

When you are fishing these remote alpine lakes it is important that you be prepared for any accidents or injuries that might happen. It is important that you are aware of the weather, terrain, your hiking abilities, plus a little common sense can help to ensure a safe and enjoyable fishing trip.

Travel with a companion. You don't want to be by yourself in case of an emergency. Leave a copy of your itinerary with a responsible person. Include such details as the make, year, and license plate of your car, the equipment you're bringing, the weather you've anticipated, and when you plan to return. Be in good physical condition. Set a comfortable pace as you hike. A group trip should be designed for the weakest member of the group. If you have any medical conditions, discuss your plans with your healthcare provider and get approval before departing. Make sure you have the skills you need for your camping or hiking adventure. You may need to know how to read a compass, erect a temporary shelter, or give first aid. Practice your skills in advance. If your trip will be strenuous, get into good physical condition before setting out. If you plan to climb or travel to high altitudes, make plans for proper acclimatization to the altitude.

Think about your footing while traveling near cliffs. Trees and bushes can't always be trusted to hold you. Stay on developed trails or dry, solid rock areas with good footing.

Wear appropriate clothing for the trail conditions and season.

Check your equipment. Keep your equipment in good working order. Inspect it before your trip. Do not wait until you are at the trailhead. Be sure to pack emergency signaling devices.

Be weather wise. Keep an eye on current and predicted weather conditions. In the Wasatch Mountains, weather can change very quickly. Know the signs for approaching storms or changing weather conditions. Avoid bare ridge tops, exposed places, lone trees, streams, and rocks during lightning storms. Find shelter in a densely forested area at a lower elevation. Even in the summer, exposure to wind and rain can result in hypothermia.

Learn basic first aid so you will know how to identify and treat injuries and illnesses. Carry a first aid kit with you. Learn how to identify the symptoms of heat exhaustion, heat stroke, hypothermia, and dehydration, and know how to treat them.

Make camp before dark. Traveling after darkness has resulted in many accidents from falls, so travel only during daylight. Set up camp well away from the edge of cliffs, and learn the terrain during daylight. If you have to leave camp after dark, stay in areas you have

263

seen in daylight, go with a friend, and always use a good flashlight.

Be alert for slippery areas and take your time to avoid tripping. Low-hanging branches and variable terrains make running unsafe, and leaves can hide slippery areas underneath.

Alcohol and cliffs don't mix! If you drink, stay away from the cliffs. Judgment, agility, and balance are all reduced by alcohol consumption.

Think before you drink! No matter how clean or pure stream water looks, it's likely to contain water-borne parasites and microorganisms that can cause discomfort and sometimes serious illness. Pack your water in, or purify through chemical treatment.

Mountain weather is generally cooler, cloudier, and windier than in lowland areas. For every 1,000 feet of elevation, the temperature often drops three to five degrees. Thus, it's best to dress in layers. Polyester clothing worn closest to your skin will trap warm air next to the skin and transfer or wick body moisture away.

Wear sunglasses and a hat or visor when you hike, ski or paddle. Snow blindness, caused by the sun's glare on snow, can also be caused by sunlight reflecting off water and boulders. Keep your eyes and face covered especially during your first few days outdoors.

Bring sunscreen no matter the season. You can get painful sunburn even in subfreezing temperatures.

Drink plenty of water. Water is heavy to carry, but thirst on the trail is a hazard. Take a tip from athletes: before a hike, drink some water so you're well hydrated and energized. Never drink your total supply between refills.

Backcountry water supplies are unpredictable. It's better to arrive at a gushing stream with 1/3 quart of water left, than to arrive at an empty stream and have no water left at all. Treat or filter all water.

Pack carbohydrate-energy bars, granola, candy, or fruit. They provide an instant pick-me-up on the trail.

Give yourself about two hour's daylight to set up camp.

Lightning

High on the list of activities where people are injured by lightning are mountain hiking, climbing, camping, fishing, boating, and golfing.

Many vacationers are unaware of the measures they can take to lower their risk of being struck. They should educate themselves about lightning strikes. They should be near safe shelter and try to avoid high terrain, golf courses, and bodies of water during high lightning activity (late morning to evening).

If you are caught above the tree line when a storm approaches, descend quickly. Avoid isolated trees. It is better to run into a forest.

Electric storms can also develop in the middle of the night. To lower your odds, don't pitch your tent near the tallest trees in the vicinity.

Hikers, fishermen and others should run into a forest if a shelter or car is not nearby.

If you are caught in an open field, seek a low spot. Crouch with your feet together and head low.

Don't sit or lie down, because these positions provide much more contact with the ground, providing a wider path for lightning to follow. If you are with a group and the threat of lightning is high, spread out at least 15 feet apart to minimize the chance of everybody getting hit (see "If Someone Is Struck").

Don't return to an open area too soon. People have been struck by lightning near the end of a storm, which is still a dangerous time.

Anglers should get off lakes or rivers and seek shelter when storms approach. Drop any fishing rods.

Essential Equipment

Pack the "Essentials" and be prepared for minor injuries, sudden weather changes or delays. The following are items you should include in your pack:

Candle

Clothing (always bring something warm, extra socks, and rain gear)

Compass

First aid kit

Food (bring extra)

Flashlight

Foil (to use as a cup or signaling device)

Hat

Insect repellent

Map

Nylon filament

Pocket knife

Pocket mirror (to use as a signaling device)

Prescription glasses (an extra pair)

Prescription medications for ongoing medical conditions

Radio with batteries

Space blanket or a piece of plastic (to use for warmth or shelter)

Sunglasses

Sunscreen

Trash bag (makes an adequate poncho)

Water

Waterproof matches or matches in a waterproof tin

Water purification tablets

Whistle (to scare off animals or to use as a signaling device)

First Aid Kit

I recommend that everyone who goes on a day hike or an overnight excursion into these mountains carry a first aid kit. I have included the most important items to have in your first aid kit. Excellent first aid kits for hiking and backpacking can be purchased at sporting good stores.

The first aid kit should be kept in a waterproof container.

First aid requires more than just having the proper materials, one also needs to have the first aid material easily accessible, know how to use it, and know when application of first aid is indicated. It's a good idea to carry a small simple pocket guide for treatment of common ailments. These are available at local sporting good stores.

Contents of a first aid kit are not cast in stone. The list should be altered as makes sense based upon conditions such as weather and terrain, or for hikers with special medical needs, like those requiring medications for allergies, cardiac or respiratory problems.

The list includes:

Triangular bandage – for slings, bandages, and splint tie-downs

Band-Aids – for small wounds

Sterile Gauze – a half dozen 4x4" for dressings

Ace bandage – support for sprains

Duct tape – for splinting, bandage

Moleskin – for blister prevention or treatment

Antiseptic wipes – to clean wounds

Antibiotic ointment – to prevent infection in wounds

Ibuprofen – anti-inflammatory

Aspirin – 300 mg crushed under tongue for heart attack symptoms

Personal medications

Roll bandages

Butterfly bandages

Sterile compresses

Adhesive tape

Sterile gauze pads

Antiseptic wipes

Twine

Tweezers

Safety pins

Scissors

Thermometer

Latex gloves

Tissues

Plastic Bags

Small mirror

Eye drops

Burn Ointment

Sunburn lotion

Disinfectant cream

Antihistamine tablets

Anti-acids

Hydrogen peroxide

Diarrhea medication

Hydrocortisone cream

Poison Ivy cream / cleansers

Bee sting kit

Snake bite kit

Heat / cold packs

First aid manual

CELL PHONE / SATELLITE PHONE / RADIOS

It is always a good idea to carry your cell phone with you when you are hiking in the Wasatch Mountains. Cell phones actually work in some areas of these mountains. The phones tend to work best along the highways and where they have line of sight capabilities. Cell phones rarely work in the bottom of canyons or in areas that limit or block cell phone signals.

Satellite Phones are expensive but the will work in most if not all areas of the Wasatch.

It is a very good idea that if you are hiking with a companion or companions that each of you carry radios in case you get separated. Like cell phones radios work well when they have line of sight capabilities. Good radios for hiking can be bought at local sporting good stores.

CHAPTER 12

CAMPGROUND AND FOREST SERVICE INFORMATION

BIG COTTONWOOD CANYON

SPRUCES CAMPGROUND

Spruces Campground is located 9.7 miles up Big Cottonwood Canyon at an elevation of 7,500 feet. Salt Lake City is conveniently close.

The campground is set among a forest of spruce and aspen trees. The campground is large and contains several group overnight campsites and day-use picnic sites, as well as numerous single and double-family campsites. All sites have picnic tables, campfire rings and grills.

Flush toilets and drinking water are provided. A baseball field, volleyball court and horseshoe pits are located within the campground. Firewood is available for purchase from the host. Roads and parking spurs are paved.

We spend many summer nights at this campground. This is a great location to beat the summer heat of the valley. Park your camper and commute to work during the day and then return in the evening just in time to catch the hatch on Big Cottonwood Creek. Evenings are cool and the stars are dazzling. Sit by the camp fire and let the stress of your day to day routine melt away. There are many campsites close to the stream. Leave your window open and be lulled to sleep by the sound of the stream.

FEES:

Current Conditions:	Check with the Forest Service before heading to campground
Reservations:	For reservations call 1-877-444-6777 or click here to make reservations on-line. Reservations must be made at least 5 days in advance.
Fees	81 Single Sites- $22.00 9 Double Sites - $44.00 2 Triple Sites - $66.00 2 Day Use Group Sites - $95.00, Capacity - 50 people 2 Overnight Group Sites - $145.00, Capacity - 50 people 2 Day Use Group Sites - $195.00, Capacity - 100 people 2 Day Use Group Sites - $210.00, Capacity - 150 people w/pavilion Day Use Hiking Access - $5.00
Restrictions:	7 day stay limit.

This campground is located Big Cottonwood Canyon, which is in the Salt Lake City Watershed. Special regulations apply and are strictly enforced. No pets allowed. This area is closed to swimming.

Water:	Drinking Water
Information Center:	For more information contact the Salt Lake Ranger District at 801-733-2660.

Campground Camping

Reservation Info	Part of the single/double and triple sites are available to reserve.
No. of Sites	30 single sites 9 double sites 2 triple sites 2 day use group sites that can accommodate up to 50 people 2 over night group sites that can accommodate up to 50 people 2 day use group sites that can accommodate up to 100 people 1 day use group site that can accommodate up to 150 people 1 day use group site that can accommodate up to 100 people w/pavilion.
No. of Accessible sites	

RV Camping

Reservation Info	Part of the single/double and triple sites are available to reserve.
No. of Sites	30 single sites 9 double sites

2 triple sites

2 day use group sites that can accommodate up to 50 people

2 over night group sites that can accommodate up to 50 people

2 day use group sites that can accommodate up to 100 people

1 day use group site that can accommodate up to 150 people

1 day use group site that can accommodate up to 100 people w/pavilion.

**No. of
Accessible sites**

Group Camping

**No. of
Sites**

2 day use group sites that can accommodate up to 50 people

2 over night group sites that can accommodate up to 50 people

2 day use group sites that can accommodate up to 100 people

1 day use group site that can accommodate up to 150 people

1 day use group site that can accommodate up to 100 people w/pavilion.

HOW TO GET THERE:

From I-215, take the 6200 South exit and travel a mile east to Wasatch Blvd. Take Wasatch Blvd a mile south to junction with Big Cottonwood Canyon/Highway 190. Make a left at the junction and travel up Big Cottonwood Canyon 9.7 miles to the campground.

REDMAN CAMPGROUND

Redman Campground is located 14 miles up Big Cottonwood Canyon at an elevation of 8,300 feet.

Just like Spruces Campground, Redman campground is set among a forest of spruce and pine trees.

The campground contains two group sites and numerous single and double-family sites, all with picnic tables and campfire rings. Flush toilets and drinking water are provided. Firewood is available for purchase from the host. Roads and parking spurs are dirt.

Current Conditions:	Check with the Forest Service

Reservations:	For reservations call 1-877-444-6777 Reservations must be made at least 5 days in advance.
Fees	32 Single Sites - $21.00 2 Double Sites - $42.00 2 Triple Sites - $63.00 1 Group Site - $95.00, Capacity -35 people 1 Group Site - $140.00, Capacity - 50 people 7 day stay limit.
Restrictions:	This campground is located Big Cottonwood Canyon, which is in the Salt Lake City Watershed. Special regulations apply and are strictly enforced. No pets allowed. This area is closed to swimming.
Water:	None
Information Center:	For more information contact the Salt Lake Ranger District at 801-733-2660.

HOW TO GET THERE:

From I-215, take the 6200 South exit and travel a mile east to Wasatch Blvd. Take Wasatch Blvd a mile south to junction with Big Cottonwood Canyon/Highway 190. Make a left at the junction and travel up Big Cottonwood Canyon for 14 miles to the campground.

JORDAN PINES GROUP CAMPSITE

Jordan Pines Campground is located 9.2 miles up Big Cottonwood Canyon at an elevation of 7500 feet.

The campground is located amongst shady pines and aspens.

This group campground is a perfect location for family reunions, church outings and company picnics. It offers four overnight campsites and one day-use picnic site, all of which contain picnic tables, campfire rings and grills.

Vault toilets and drinking water are provided. Volleyball court and horseshoe pits are available, but campers must bring their own net, ball and horseshoes. Roads and parking spurs are paved.

Park Season	Site Type	Nightly/Daily Rates
Peak Season May 23 2014 - Sep 01 2014	GROUP TENT ONLY AREA NONELECTRIC	$220.00
	GROUP STANDARD NONELECTRIC	$220.00-$265.00
	GROUP PICNIC AREA	$110.00

HOW TO GET THERE:
From I-215, take the 6200 south exit and travel a mile east to Wasatch Blvd. Take Wasatch Blvd a mile south to junction with Big Cottonwood Canyon/Highway 190. Make a left at the junction and travel up Big Cottonwood Canyon 9.2 miles to the campground.

LITTLE COTTONWOOD CANYON

TANNERS FLAT CAMPGROUND

Tanners Flat Campground is located 4.1 miles up Little Cottonwood Canyon at an elevation of 7,200 feet.

The campground is set among a forest of shady pine, aspen, oak and maple trees. Little Cottonwood Creek runs along the edge of the campground.

The campground contains seven accessible group sites and

numerous single and double-family sites, all with picnic tables and campfire rings. Group sites also have grills and serving tables.

Flush and vault toilets are provided, as is drinking water. A volleyball court is available but campers must bring their own net and ball. Firewood is available for purchase from the host. Roads and parking spurs are paved.

Current Conditions:	Open for the 2013 season.
Reservations:	For reservations call 1-877-444-6777 Reservations must be made at least 5 days in advance.
Fees	31 Single Sites - $22.00 3 Double Sites - $44.00 3 Group Sites - $80.00, Capacity - 25 People 1 Group Site - $125.00, Capacity - 50 people 1 Amphitheater for 4-hour blocks - $50.00, Capacity - 70 people 7 day stay limit.
Restrictions:	This campground is located Little Cottonwood Canyon, which is in the Salt Lake City Watershed. Special regulations apply and are strictly enforced. No pets allowed. This area is closed to swimming.
Water:	Drinking Water
Information Center:	For more information contact the Salt Lake Ranger District at 801-733-2660.

Campground Camping

Reservation Info	Reservations must be made at least 5 days in advance for July 24 through September 1.
No. of Sites	31 single sites

3 double sites
3 group sites that can accommodate up to 25 people
1 group site that can accommodate up to 50 people
1 amphitheater that can accommodate up to 70 people (4 hr blocks)

No. of Accessible sites   21 single sites, 1 double sites and 1 triple site.

RV Camping

Reservation Info   Reservations must be made at least 5 days in advance for July 24 through September 1.

No. of Sites
31 single sites
3 double sites
3 group sites that can accommodate up to 25 people
1 group site that can accommodate up to 50 people
1 amphitheater that can accommodate up to 70 people (4 hr blocks)

HOW TO GET THERE:

From I-215, take the 6200 South exit and travel a mile east to Wasatch Blvd. Take Wasatch Blvd 3 miles south to junction with Little Cottonwood Canyon/Highway 210. Take a left at the junction and travel up Little Cottonwood Canyon for 4.1 miles to the campground.

ALBION BASIN CAMPGROUND

Albion Basin Campground is LOCATED 10.2 miles up Little Cottonwood Canyon and is situated among shady white pines and aspens at an elevation of 9,500 feet.

Albion Basin is a favorite location for people to view wildflowers in July. Moose and deer frequent the basin and mountain goats can often be seen on the cliffs.

Current Conditions:	Check with the Forest Service before heading to campground
Reservations:	For reservations call 1-877-444-6777 or click here to make reservations on-line.

	Reservations must be made at least 5 days in advance.
Area Amenities:	Tent camping, Picnic tables,Toilets, Drinking water
Fees	16 Single Sites - $19.00 2 Double Sites $38.00 1 Triple Site $57.00
Restrictions:	7 day stay limit.
Water:	Drinking Water
Restroom:	Vault
Information Center:	For more information contact the Salt Lake Ranger District at 801-733-2660.

Campground Camping

Reservation Info

No. of Sites	16 single sites 2 double sites 1 triple site

HOW TO GET THERE:

From I-215, take the 6200 South exit and travel a mile east to Wasatch Blvd. Take Wasatch Blvd 3 miles south to the junction with Little Cottonwood Canyon/Highway 210. Take a left at the junction and travel up Little Cottonwood Canyon 10.2 miles to the campground. The last 2.4 miles are on a maintained gravel road.

AMERICAN FORK CANYON

LITTLE MILL CAMPGROUND

Little Mill Campground is located 4 miles up American Fork Canyon on the banks of American Fork Creek. This popular campground is a great place to escape the hot summer days while hiking or fishing. Little Mill campground is also close enough to both the Provo and Salt Lake metro areas to allow people to stay at the campground in the evening and then go to work during the day.

The campground is situated among dense stands of aspen, oak and maple trees, which provide nice shade and beautiful autumn color. Wildlife and summer wildflowers are abundant.

The campground contains one group site and several family sites, many of which are accessible. Vault toilets, fire pits, and picnic tables are provided.

Reservations:	To reserve a campsite call 1-877-444-6777
	Reservations need to be made 5 days in advance.
	34 single sites-$18.00, capacity - 8
	2 double sites-$36.00, capacity - 16
Fees	1 group site-$150.00, capacity - 50
	A per vehicle per day extra vehicle fee will be collected on site-$7.00
	7 day stay limit
Restrictions:	Off-highway vehicles (roller blades, bicycles, skate boards and scooters are not allowed in the campground. Gates close at 10 pm.
Closest Towns:	American Fork, UT.
Water:	None
Restroom:	Flush
	Campers must have a recreation pass before camping.
	Three-day passes are $6 per vehicle
	Seven day passes are $12 per vehicle
	Annual passes are $45 per vehicle
Passes:	Passes are available at entrance stations located on either side of the Alpine Scenic Loop or 3 day passes can be purchased at self service fee tubes located at major trail heads. Recreation pass and vehicle fee will be collected at the Fee Demo Booth at the mouth of the American Fork Canyon.
Information Center:	For more information contact the Pleasant Grove Ranger District at 801-785-3563.

Campground Camping

Fire Information These campsites have fire rings.

Reservation Info Part of the single sites are available to reserve.

289

No. of Sites	34 Single sites
	2 Double sites
	1 Group sites that can accommodate up to 50 people

RV Camping

Reservation Info	Part of the single sites are available to reserve.
Fire Information	These campsites have fire rings.

No. of Sites	34 Single sites
	2 Double sites
	1 Group site that can accommodate up to 50 people
Size Restrictions	Size restrictions vary between 35 - 60 feet.
Pavement Type for Parking	Paved

HOW TO GET THERE:

From Salt Lake City or Provo, take I-15 to the Alpine-Highland exit 284. Travel 8 miles east on Utah Highway 92 to the mouth of American Fork Canyon. Stay on 92 for 4 miles to the campground.

GRANITE FLAT
CAMPGROUND

Granite Flat Campground is located about 7 miles up scenic American Fork Canyon, less than a mile from Tibble Fork Reservoir. Campers can enjoy fishing, canoeing and hiking local trails.

The campground is situated among dense stands of aspen, Douglas fir, spruce and pine trees at an elevation of 6,400 feet.

This large campground offers three group sites and several single and double-family sites, most of which are accessible. Picnic tables and campfire rings are provided, as are vault toilets and drinking water.
Roads and parking spurs are paved.
TIBBLE FORK AND SILVER FLAT RESERVOIRS ARE CLOSE AND OFFER GREAT FISHING OPPORTUNITIES.

Current   Check with Forest Service before heading up to

Conditions:	camp.
Reservations:	To reserve a campsite call 1-877-444-6777 Reservations must be made 5 days in advance.
Area Amenities:	Picnic tables
Fees	44 single sites-$18.00, capacity - 8 people + 1 vehicle per single site 8 double sites-$36.00, capacity - 16 2 group sites-$190.00, capacity - 100 1 group site-$215.00, capacity - 125 An extra vehicle fee will be collected per vehicle per day on site-$7.00 7 day stay limit
Restrictions:	No all-terrain or off-highway vehicles allowed in the campground. Gate closes at 10pm. Check local boating restrictions, there are a number of areas that are close by that boats are prohibited.
Closest Towns:	American Fork, UT.
Water:	Drinking Water
Restroom:	Vault
Passes:	Campers must have a recreation pass before camping. Three-day passes are $6 per vehicle Seven day passes are $12 per vehicle Annual passes are $45 per vehicle Passes are available at entrance stations located on either side of the Alpine Scenic Loop or 3 day passes can be purchased at self service fee tubes located at major trail heads.
Information Center:	For more information contact the Pleasant Grove Ranger District at 801-785-3563.

Campground Camping

Reservation Info	Part of the single/double sites and the group sites are available to reserve.
Fire Information	These campsites have fire rings.
No. of Sites	44 Single sites 8 Double sites 2 Group sites that can accommodate up to 100 people 1 Group site that can accommodate up to 125 people

RV Camping

Reservation Info	Part of the single/double sites and the group sites are available to reserve.
Fire Information	These campsites have fire rings.
No. of Sites	44 Single sites 8 Double sites 2 Group sites that can accommodate up to 100 people 1 Group site that can accommodate up to 125 people
Size Restrictions	Size restrictions vary between 20-45 feet.
Pavement Type for Parking	Paved

Group Camping

Fire Information	These campsites have fire rings.
Reservation Info	Group sites are available to reserve.
No. of Sites	

2 Group sites that can accommodate up to 100 people
1 Group site that can accommodate up to 125 people

HOW TO GET THERE:

From Salt Lake City, Utah, take I-15 to the Alpine-Highland exit 284. Go east on Highway 92 for 8 miles to mouth of American Fork Canyon. Go 5 miles up the canyon to junction; take the North Fork/Forest Road 85 to Tibble Fork Reservoir. Stay left on paved road for a mile to the campground.

NOTES

*NOTE – Wildlife photography is courtesy of the Utah Division of Wildlife Resources

*NOTE – Illustrations of fish species in this book are credited to the Utah Department of Wildlife Services.

*NOTE - Fish pictures, fish stocking plane, fish stocking truck and picture of Tiger Salamander are credited to the Utah Division of Wildlife resource.

*NOTE – Topographic maps were obtained through http://mapserv.utah.gov/raster/?catGroup=24K%20DRG,100K%20DRG,250K%20DRG&title=USGS%20Topo%20Maps. Topo maps were edited by the author.

*NOTE - Aerial photography and digital orthophotography acquired by the USDA are in the public domain and are available to federal and state agencies, and to the general public through the Aerial Photography Field Office. Aerial maps were edited by author.

*NOTE – Information regarding the campgrounds located in the Wasatch National Forest was obtained from the USDA Forest Service site.

*NOTE – Information regarding bear safety, cougar safety and safety in the backcountry is credited to the Utah Department of Wildlife Resources and the United States Forest Service.

Made in United States
Troutdale, OR
04/23/2024

19397534R00166